Praise for *So What?*

"This book shows you how to make an instant connection based on trust and respect with each person you meet, faster and easier than you ever thought possible."

—**Brian Tracy**, Author of *The Power of Charm*

"Sometimes the simplest ideas are the most powerful. I wish I had read *So What?* earlier in my sales career."

—**Ed Cosgrove**, EMC New Hire Program Manager

"Everything you want exists just beyond your comfort zone. The So What Mindset will help you get there and make this new way of thinking a part of your daily experience."

—**Robert Kiltz M.D.**, Founder and Director, CNY Fertility Center

"Whether talking with one person or addressing 1000, everyone can benefit from learning how to more effectively deliver our messages. *So What?* offers a simple, profound process that leads to quickly developing rapport and connecting with one's listeners—every time!"

—**Barbara A. Culver**, CFP, ChFC, CLU, AEP, Resonate, Inc., Purposeful Planning

"Mark Magnacca's message is important for everyone, but especially for those of us in the financial services industry. In today's environment, knowing how to communicate effectively with clients is essential for their benefit and for ours. For example, ask yourself whether you've adequately explained to your clients the concept of risk...then go out and buy this book."

—**Geoff Davey**, President, FinaMetrica

"In today's ever-competitive world, it is not enough to offer a superior service. You need superior communications skills so your message gets out. Mark Magnacca helps you be heard with the advice in his effective new book *So What?*"

—**Richard Ferri**, CEO Portfolios Solutions, LLC

"*So What?* delivers! It's about time we have a book that shows us step-by-step how to act on the wisdom that 'It's all about the customer (or audience or prospect), not us.' In clear, concrete, and compelling language, Mark Magnacca guides us in crafting the message that authentically links our offerings to the audience's real needs and leads them to say 'Tell me more.' Read this book, cut through the complexity of client courtship, gain more of your ideal customers, and enjoy your work. That's the So What Benefit!"

—**Ed Jacobson**, Ph.D., Author of *Appreciative Moments: Stories and Practices for Living and Working Appreciatively*

So What?

So What?

How to Communicate What Really Matters to Your Audience

Mark Magnacca

FT Press offers excellent discounts on this book when ordered in quantity for bulk purchases or special sales. For more information, please contact U.S. Corporate and Government Sales, 1-800-382-3419, corpsales@pearsontechgroup. com. For sales outside the U.S., please contact International Sales at international@pearson. com.

Seventh Printing October 2010

ISBN-10: 0-13-715826-2
ISBN-13: 978-0-13-715826-3

Pearson Education LTD.
Pearson Education Australia PTY, Limited.
Pearson Education Singapore, Pte. Ltd.
Pearson Education North Asia, Ltd.
Pearson Education Canada, Ltd.
Pearson Educación de Mexico, S.A. de C.V.
Pearson Education—Japan
Pearson Education Malaysia, Pte. Ltd.

Library of Congress Cataloging-in-Publication Data

Magnacca, Mark, 1969-
  So what : how to communicate what really matters to your audience / Mark Magnacca. -- 1st ed.
      p. cm.
  ISBN 978-0-13-715826-3 (hardback : alk. paper) 1. Business communication. 2. Interpersonal communication. I. Title.
  HF5718.M34 2009
  808.5'1--dc22
                                    2008054619

Vice President, Publisher
Tim Moore

Associate Publisher and Director of Marketing
Amy Neidlinger

Acquisitions Editor
Jennifer Simon

Editorial Assistant
Pamela Boland

Operations Manager
Gina Kanouse

Digital Marketing Manager
Julie Phifer

Publicity Manager
Laura Czaja

Assistant Marketing Manager
Megan Colvin

Cover Designer
Chuti Prasertsith

Managing Editor
Kristy Hart

Project Editor
Jovana San Nicolas-Shirley

Copy Editor
Water Crest Publishing

Proofreader
Sheri Cain

Indexer
Lisa Stumpf

Compositor
Nonie Ratcliff

Manufacturing Buyer
Dan Uhrig

This book is dedicated to my wife and soulmate Kristen.
As my trusted advisor, she has helped me to understand what really matters. I am grateful for her unwavering support, incredible intuition, and help in understanding the power of changing the question from "What's in it for me?" to "What's in it for them?"

In memory of Jeff Goldberg, who helped change my trajectory by caring enough to ask "So what?"

In memory of Richard B. Ross, whose life exemplified what's possible when you have a So What Mindset.

CONTENTS

ABOUT THE AUTHOR

Mark Magnacca has invested the past 15 years on a search for what sets great communicators apart.

So What? is the result of five years of work simplifying this powerful idea to book form. Each idea has been tested in his own life and business, as well as with a wide range of clients. Mark's unique ability to bring these ideas to life will enable you to easily understand them and apply them in your own life.

As founder and president of Insight Development Group, Inc., his seminar and training programs have been featured in *The New York Times*, *USA Today*, and on CNN's *MoneyLine*. Mark has helped thousands of entrepreneurs, salespeople, and executives adopt a So What Mindset that makes them indispensable in any economic cycle.

Mark lives on Cape Cod, Massachusetts, with his wife Kristen and two children. A graduate of Babson College, Mark is the author of *The Product Is You* and is a participant in the Strategic Coach Master's Program.

FOREWORD

You are holding in your hands a book that offers you a new way of thinking, which will make you indispensable in any economic environment. It is also a book where the concepts and principles have already been proven and tested.

Mark called me some ten years ago after reading my book, *Inspire Any Audience*, and said, "I want you to be my coach." I love, as he does, coaching those who want to win, who want to experience more, and who want to expand their value. Year after year, I've seen him study the subject of presenting and become one of the best presentation coaches I know.

Mark has a unique ability to coach and present in a way that makes the application of tools and techniques intuitive. In fact, of all the people I've coached over the last 25 years—more than 1,000 people, who include presidents of Wal-Mart, Sam's Club, Samsung, Ford, EDS, and Shell—there has been no one quite like Mark. One of the great joys of being a coach is seeing your "players" win. This has been part of the joy for me: watching Mark grow and leverage his expertise to help so many others.

Although there have been countless communication/ presentation/"think differently" books, there has never been one that focuses as clearly and as simply on the two questions that are most important to any audience. Many of these other books say to focus on the needs of the person doing the talking. This book says the only thing that matters is what is important to the person doing the listening.

The most effective leaders, politicians, and executives know how to do this. They always answer the implicit So What Question every time they communicate.

Let me encourage you to get out your highlighter and put on your thinking cap so that you can learn from and enjoy this book. Highlight the key points, study each page, and share the tools and ideas with your team and colleagues. Sign up for the 21-day challenge in Chapter 10, "Getting From Where You Are to Where You Want to Be," and help make these ideas a part of who you are.

Treasure this book, put it into practice, and watch for many great results to come your way.

—Tony Jeary—Mr. Presentation™
Coach to the World's Top CEOs

"SHARPEN YOUR INTEREST IN TWO MAJOR SUBJECTS: LIFE AND PEOPLE. YOU WILL ONLY GATHER INFORMATION FROM A SOURCE IF YOU ARE INTERESTED IN IT."
—JIM ROHN

CHAPTER 1
WHAT YOU NEED TO KNOW IN 850 WORDS

The people you are trying to communicate with, sell to, or reach don't really care about you, or what you have to offer, until they know how what you have can benefit them.

If you keep that in mind every time you make a speech, do a sales presentation, write a client a memo, or simply talk to someone in the hallway, you will do the following:

- ▶ Engage your audience because you are more relevant.

- ▶ Make more money.

- ▶ Get what you want in life.

In other words, if you help enough people get what they want, by showing or explaining how what you have can benefit them, you can have anything you want.

It's that simple. But don't let the simplicity fool you. This is a seductively straightforward idea that up until now has been very difficult to actually apply.

The reason? Most of us have not been trained to think this way. We've been taught when it comes to communicating, "it is all about us" rather than "it's all about them." We often think it's all about the words

we use, the way we look, and showing how smart
we are.

As a result, when we talk to people, we say (directly or
otherwise), "I'm going to tell you about my product,
my service, my idea, my campaign."

During much of the twentieth century, that approach
worked pretty well. The people we were talking to had
a limited number of options when it came to getting
information, and so they were willing to put up with
a lot, since the alternative—going to the library or
making lots of phone calls—was difficult.

But that was then. Today, when anyone can find just
about anything with just a couple of clicks on a search
engine like Google, that way of thinking is hopelessly
outdated.

This is not to say that making your message all
about you never works. You may be able to think of
examples where somebody talked about themselves
and only what was important to them, and you were
still interested. But that said, I bet you can't come up
with many.

In the pages ahead, you will see how people like
George Lucas, Ronald Reagan, Steve Jobs, and John
F. Kennedy instinctively used the So What Question
to their advantage—and ours. They focused on what

was important to their audience and were remarkably effective as a result.

You might be thinking, "How can I possibly do what any of them have done?" Well, that's where I come in.

You are going to learn ten ways to apply this powerful idea that will help you automatically change the way you communicate with people, from "here's-what-I-want-to-have-happen" to "here's-how-my-message-can-benefit-you (my audience)."

I will show you how to stay on track by focusing on what matters most to your audience, so they quickly understand the benefit to them and what you are offering.

The net result of reading this book is that you will instinctively know the best way to communicate your message to engage your audience so that they want to follow you.

I wish I could tell you that the ideas I will be sharing with you are something I always knew and used. But that's not true. In fact, I have come to understand the power of the **So What Question** based on studying my own mistakes, as well as the communication mistakes—and successes—of people who have helped change our world.

PRACTICING WHAT I PREACH

This book is organized in a way that is designed to benefit you most. Each chapter will help you understand **WHY** the So What Question matters in your life and business, and then give you specific tools to show you **HOW** to apply what you've learned. Read this book in any order you choose—cover to cover, or skipping around to solve a specific problem you may have, or any way in between.

No matter how you read this book, by the time you are done, you will come to understand that if you can anticipate—and address—the So What Question that is always in your audience's mind, you will be much more successful in business and in life. (Yep, the So What Question works in more than just your business.)

I realize this seems like a big promise, but what I will be sharing with you has already been tested on people just like you—people who had goals they wanted to accomplish, products and services they wanted to sell, income they wanted to generate, and ideas they wanted to become reality.

They succeeded.

And you can, too.

Let's begin.

TAKE-AWAY IDEAS

1. The people you are trying to communicate with, sell to, or reach don't really care about you, or what you have to offer, until they know how what you have can benefit them.

2. I want to tell you about my product, my service, my campaign…. This approach worked in the twentieth century, but is now outdated.

3. Adopt this new way of thinking…and the payoff will be an engaged audience, more money, and getting what you want in life.

"WHEN YOU CHANGE THE WAY YOU LOOK AT THINGS, THE THINGS YOU LOOK AT CHANGE."
—WAYNE DYER

CHAPTER 2
CHANGE YOUR THINKING, CHANGE YOUR LIFE

It is the most recognized opening of any movie ever created. *Star Wars* begins with these words flowing across the screen: "A long time ago, in a galaxy far, far away…" and immediately you are into the story of how a simple farm boy, aided by a few newly met allies, tries to save the universe (and a beautiful princess) from a psychopathic emperor.

But if the Directors Guild of America (DGA) had their way, we never would have had that opening.

Instead, we would have seen a series of credits like names of the director, the writer, the actors, and key members of the production staff. Only then would the story have gotten underway. Union rules required the credits to come first.

It would be hard to think of a more boring way to begin an action movie.

Director George Lucas (who also wrote the movie) knew that. That's why he lobbied (successfully) the DGA for special permission to create this memorable opening.

George Lucas broke the existing rules and conventional mindset that pervaded the thinking of the movie business at that time. Like a Jedi knight, Lucas had mastered the **So What Mindset**—the idea that the needs of his audience always came first. As a result, he changed the way people think about the ways movies are made.[1]

According to *Forbes* magazine in 2005, the overall revenue generated by the entire *Star Wars* franchise over the course of its 28-year history was nearly $20 billion, easily making it one of the most successful film series of all time and George Lucas one of the most successful directors and entrepreneurs of all time. I want to be clear that I am not saying that having credits at the beginning of a movie is necessarily wrong. By way of contrast, the second most profitable film franchise, the James Bond movies, included (black and white) credits at the beginning of every movie; however, the way the opening is structured with music, imagery, and the famous gunshot (where the screen turns red) allows the James Bond series to capture audience attention in a very different, but still relevant, fashion.

---

[1] In one of the great ironies of all time, when he completed the sequel to *Star Wars*, the film *The Empire Strikes Back*, Lucas assumed he would be granted permission to do the same thing with the credits as he did initially—that is, save them for the end of the movie. He was wrong. Not only did the DGA *not* grant permission, but they also fined him and his director (Irvin Kershner) $250,000 and threatened to sue to prevent the opening of the film. Lucas paid the fines but quit the DGA, deciding it was more important for him to give the audience the best experience possible.

The point is that there are many ways of applying the So What Mindset, but the strategy behind the So What Mindset is always the same—namely that you must put the needs of your audience first, no matter what you are selling, be it a product, service, or movie.

The tactics you use to execute this strategy may be as different as the opening credits in *Star Wars* or a James Bond movie, but the strategy itself always remains the same.

IT KEEPS YOU CURRENT

One of the key benefits to adopting the So What Mindset is the ability to help you stay relevant even as times change. Let's stick with the discussion of movies to make the point.

Lawrence of Arabia—winner of seven Academy Awards, including Best Picture—begins with a four-minute overture and has an intermission after the first two hours. (The film runs almost four.)

When this movie was first released in 1962, sitting in the theater and waiting four minutes may have been appropriate. Watching that movie today, staring at a black screen for four minutes while listening to music —even music as good as Maurice Jarre's (who won an Oscar for it)—seems like an eternity.

Not even the most clueless movie director would begin a film this way today. Literally, there is no way an audience would sit still for it.

Speaking of the importance of music, in 1984, the movie *Against All Odds* was released and flopped at the box office. Interestingly, the theme song by Phil Collins was one of the biggest hits that year. Most people had left the theater before they heard the song because it played at the end of the movie rather than at the beginning. Why did the music come in at the end of the credits? Because one of the producers loved the idea of using the song to sum up the movie.

Would putting the song first have helped sell tickets? We will never know. But we do know movies such as *Flashdance* and *Grease* were likely hits because of their music.

Why is the discussion about movie credits and music important to you? Because it's easy to fall into the trap of doing something—like putting a great song at the end of the movie—because *we* like it rather than thinking about what's important to the people who will buy a ticket, write a check, or otherwise consume your message.

George Lucas knew this, and now so do you.

Why should you adopt it? That's simple. You picked up this book because either:

A. You are dissatisfied with some element of the way your communication is currently received.

B. You are satisfied with your skill as a communicator, and yet you know you could be better.

In either case, in the next chapter, you'll learn about the origin of *So What?* and how it transformed my world.

TAKE-AWAY IDEAS

1. Ask yourself the same question George Lucas did when communicating with your audience… what is best for them?

2. Remember, there are multiple ways of applying the So What Mindset. James Bond had credits in the beginning of the movie, and it worked. The strategy is always the same—namely, that you must put the needs of your audience first.

3. Don't fall into the trap of doing something just because *you* like it—consider first what's important to your audience.

"THERE ARE THREE
TYPES OF PEOPLE:
THOSE WHO MAKE IT
HAPPEN, THOSE WHO
WATCH IT HAPPEN, AND
THOSE WHO WONDER
WHAT HAPPENED."
—JEFF GOLDBERG,
EXECUTIVE VICE
PRESIDENT, EMC CORP.

CHAPTER 3
How I Learned to Think
This Way—You Can, Too!

I am reluctant to admit this, but I learned about the importance of the So What Question the hard way. A client made me realize I needed help.

Let me tell you what happened so that you'll understand why:

1. Having a So What Mindset is so important.

2. If you use it, you'll have a huge competitive edge.

3. I certainly didn't have all the answers when I began—although I certainly believed I did.

4. You don't need to make the same mistakes I did and can avoid a lot of pain, suffering, and (as you will see) embarrassment.

After years of training salespeople as a professional speaker and facilitator, I felt extremely confident that I was at the top of my game—and I had testimonials from people who had heard me present to prove it. In early 1995, I received a call from Jeff Goldberg, executive vice president of EMC, the world's leading developer and provider of information infrastructure technology and solutions, who wanted to know more about my seminar program that he had read about in a local newspaper. Unbeknownst to me, Jeff was responsible for helping to reposition EMC from a small computer storage company to the number one player in their category in terms of marketshare. I met with Jeff and explained how my program worked, and he said he would get back to me after he discussed the program with his team.

He called me the following week, and I was surprised when he asked me to meet with him a second time. When I asked why, he said he wanted me to run through the presentation I planned to make to his team. He said I needed to give my speech in his office to an audience of one—him—just as I would to his sales force.

My first thought was, "Is he kidding? Why is he going to have me, in essence, audition before agreeing to hire me?"

I took a deep breath and said, "Jeff, of course. I would be glad to run through my speech with you. But can I ask you why?"

"Sure. I want to make sure that what you are going to say is relevant to my team."

Oops.

The second he said it, I realized I had never thought about whether my content was relevant to his people or not.

Now, in retrospect, I grant you that sounds simply stupid. But the only thing I can say in my meager defense is that:

1. Almost no one else was wondering about it either. Most presentations were one-way and passive: The person doing the talking delivered his message, as effectively as possible, and the recipient(s) just listened. It was the "Me Tarzan. You Jane." approach to communication.

2. Back before the web, and search engines like Google, it was difficult to learn anything about your audience ahead of time. You had to spend time in the library or make countless calls to find someone who knew something about the people you would be talking to.

3. I had a message that worked. True, I knew (as you probably do, too) I could be communicating better, but I rationalized that away by saying, "Why fix what isn't broken?"

And so, my preparing for any kind of interaction was based on coming up with vivid examples that would make my points and making sure that my opening story was funny. In fact, until Jeff asked the question, I never thought in any detail about the needs of the audience...or even what they actually did for a living.

How do you sell technology infrastructure solutions, anyway?

Stalling for time, I said to Jeff, "I can't do this justice delivering it only to you."

"Why not?"

I had no good answer and decided I had better stop making excuses. We set a time for the following week when I would present to Jeff.

It was strange presenting to just one person, but I went through it from beginning to end, while Jeff sat on the other side of his desk taking the occasional note.

When I was done, I took a sip of water and asked him, "So, what do you think?"

Jeff replied, "What's the purpose of your presentation?"

"To help salespeople stretch their comfort zone."

"Okay. But so what? Why should they care about that? What is stretching their comfort zone going to do for them?"

For the second time in the brief time I knew him, Jeff had left me speechless with one of his questions. As I thought through what he had asked, I realized Jeff wanted me to totally rethink the way I communicated.

He was (strongly) proposing that I concentrate on what my audience needed to hear, as opposed to just what I wanted to say.

I was so stunned by his suggestion that I just stared at him for a moment. I had never spent much time thinking about my communications from the audience's point of view.

After I got over the shock, I realized he was absolutely right. Of course, I would be more effective if I could show his sales force how they could benefit from my message. Helping them succeed would help me succeed as well.

I paused. I took a deep breath and tried to rethink everything I had been planning to say from the perspective of his sales force. At this moment, I realized I didn't know the answer to his question, "What's the purpose of the presentation?" I quickly realized I had to take a new approach and ask for help. I asked Jeff, "What do you believe is the biggest challenge your sales people face in terms of being able to hit their respective goals?"

Jeff paused and replied, "Complacency."

I then asked, "Can you tell me more about what you mean?"

He said, "It's easy to rest on our laurels when you've had the kind of success we've had over the last few years. What's made this company great has been the entrepreneurial spirit that causes people to go the extra mile for our customers and take nothing for granted."

"Jeff, the reality is that the biggest challenge your team faces, based on what you've told me, is complacency. This seminar is designed to remind your people of what they are capable of when they push themselves beyond their comfort zone."

I could see he was listening, but it was clear based on the expression on his face that he still wasn't sold.

"All right," he said. "That's true, but still, so what? What benefits are they going to receive if they do push themselves?"

I didn't realize it at the time, but Jeff was asking me to go further. Reduced to its absolute essence, he wanted to know, what the real value of my message was for the audience and how it was going to help them overcome complacency.

I paused and said, "Jeff, thanks for helping me understand that challenge. I believe the only way your sales team is going to hit the goals you've set for them is if they change their mindset and get outside their comfort zone. This seminar is going to help them do that by giving them a specific strategy, powerful stories, as well as the tools and techniques to help ensure they don't take their customers for granted."

Jeff finally smiled.

"Now I understand what's in it for them and what's in it for me," he said. "Make those points explicit during your talk, and you are good to go."

What I finally understood, as I started to work on my revised presentation (one that was going to be tailored to answer the So What Questions that were uppermost in the minds of the EMC sales force who would be listening to me) is that most of us know the answer to the So What Question, but we fail to address it when we communicate because of :

- ▶ **Complacency.** (Hey, I had a perfectly good speech that had worked for years.) We get into the habit of doing things the same way.

- ▶ **Self-focus.** Because we are concentrating so hard on what we are trying to say, we forget the needs of our audience.

- ▶ **Lack of curiosity.** We would rather concentrate on ourselves as opposed to them.

Thinking about all this, I was reminded of what Harvard Business School Professor Ted Levitt used to say: "People don't go to the hardware store to buy a quarter-inch drill. They go because they want to make quarter-inch holes."

I had been so busy trying to sell EMC my "version of the drill" that I had forgotten all about what they "wanted the drill for."

In my revised speech, I concentrated on making sure my audience knew what was in it for them.

So, did my new approach work?

You bet. By the time I was done with my presentation, the EMC sales force understood that to get to where they wanted to be—the industry leader—couldn't be accomplished with just more incremental effort.

Radical change was needed. (And the rest of the talk was spent explaining what kind and how.)

The EMC presentation was such a hit that I was asked back to talk to the next group of new hires. And I have used the approach of answering the So What Question in every talk I have given since.

Ten years and over 10,000 people later, the message I created was still relevant at EMC because of the So What Question—even if I had to be embarrassed into learning how powerful the So What Mindset actually is.

TAKE-AWAY IDEAS

1. **Complacency.** No matter how good a communicator you are, be willing to think about things in a new way if you've gotten into the habit of doing things the same way.

2. **Self-focus.** Beware of concentrating so hard on what you are trying to say that you forget the needs of your audience.

3. **Lack of curiosity.** Developing an inquisitive mind will translate into a genuine interest in addressing the needs of your audience. ("Here's how you, Ms. EMC Salesperson, will be able to make more money, as a result of what I have to say" as compared to the less effective approach of saying, "Let me tell you what has worked for me.")

"WHAT WE THINK
OF AS THE MOMENT
OF DISCOVERY
IS REALLY THE
DISCOVERY OF THE
RIGHT QUESTION."
—JONAS SALK

CHAPTER 4
YOUR WORLD VIEW—MAKING
THE INVISIBLE VISIBLE

Several years ago, I walked into a store looking to buy a pair of sunglasses.

The sales clerk asked me if I preferred polarized lenses.

I told him I didn't know what the difference was. He pointed to a poster on the wall and asked me to look at it with my existing, non-polarized sunglasses and tell him what I saw.

I said it looked like a piece of coral against a gray background.

Next, he gave me the polarized sunglasses and asked me to look at the same poster. I could not believe my eyes! The poster had been transformed into a tropical coral reef with blue water and brightly colored fish. It was there all the time, but I just couldn't see it.

The clerk explained that the polarized filter contained within the glass would enable me to see more vivid colors when I was outside, and I would, for example, be able to see some fish in the water that typically would not be visible with non-polarized sunglasses.

I was still a bit skeptical, but bought the glasses anyway.

I will never forget walking to the beach the first time I put them on. The same New England beach that I had been to just the day before all of a sudden looked like one in the Caribbean. The typically dark blue/green water of Cape Cod Bay suddenly shimmered with turquoise and light blue. I could even see the different colors as the water changed in depth!

When I removed my glasses, all those beautiful images disappeared.

What does this have to do with you? It's simple. The So What Filter—much like the filter contained in my polarized lenses—changes your world view and enables you to see information in a new way.

Employing the **So What Filter** will enable you to see the benefit to the person you are interacting with as clearly as I could see the coral reef and fish. As a result, you will begin to quickly understand how to organize your information in such a way that your audience will instantly understand what's in it for them.

Here's an example. For many years, I have worked as a presentation coach helping people make their message more relevant and effective. To understand exactly where they might need help, I always begin my two-day class by having them give me a brief three-minute presentation with the following set-up: Assume you typically have 20 minutes to give your "pitch," but the client has said because of a change in the schedule, you now have just three minutes. Although this is a difficult challenge for most people, it's very effective at demonstrating that when we are under pressure, we tend to revert to talking about our product and its features rather than communicating what's in it for the audience.

What I always find remarkable is how many people do just what I did with Jeff Goldberg (that is, never consider the needs of their audience before they get up to talk). They either parrot the sales pitch they were taught or present information that puts them in the best light ("I am among the company's highest producers; I was the third best-selling salesman at our company last year; I've been doing this for 18 years.") without ever questioning whether these comments would be relevant to the intended audience.

At one session, I was working with a group of investment salespeople whose goal was to persuade a group of financial advisors that their investment was a better fit for the advisor's clients than the products they currently used.

The first presentation was typical. I set the timer for three minutes, and the first student, Mike, began with, "Thank you for your time today. I want to begin by telling you about my company, my product, and myself. My company was founded in 1858, and we now have more than 5,000 employees worldwide. Also, we have recently won a customer satisfaction award, and we have been named one of the best places to work in America...."

As soon as I heard this, I couldn't help but think, "So what? Why is this relevant to me or anyone else in his target market?" He had three minutes and wasted almost a third of his time on those statements?

After the presentation, I coached Mike about the things he had done well and what he could improve for his next presentation the following morning.

I asked Mike, "Is a company that was founded in 1845 better than one founded in 1858? Because that's when your leading competitor was founded."

Mike said," I don't know," but he got the point: When your company was founded is not the critical piece of information. Rather, the goal is to explain why this is important to your audience.

I then said, "Your biggest competitor has 10,000 employees, which makes them twice as big as you. Is that good or bad?" He said, "I'm not sure, but I guess once you have over 1,000 people, it doesn't matter. You are pretty big."

I then said, "I think it's great that your company has been named one of the best places to work, but unless I am applying for a job there, why is that relevant to me as a member of your audience?"

The more questions I asked, the more color drained from Mike's face. I knew exactly what he was feeling. I remembered the sick feeling in the pit of my stomach when Jeff Goldberg asked me the same questions some ten years earlier, and I didn't have a good answer then, either. However, Jeff's questions did motivate me to think again about the purpose of my communication, and fortunately my questions to Mike caused the same reaction in him.

What happened next was telling. I asked Mike to redesign his presentation using a new technique called the **So What Matrix**. I explained that this tool would help him to transform his presentation with three simple questions:

- ▶ **For What?** For what reason are you giving the presentation?

- ▶ **So What?** Why is this important to my audience?

- ▶ **Now What?** What do you want to have happen as a result of this presentation?

As my students used the So What Matrix as a model to organize their ideas, words that were previously thought to be critical fell away. In fact, I offered each of them a highlighter and gave them the printed transcript of their own words from the presentation the day before and asked them to mark only those words or phrases that answered For What? So What? Now What?. On average, less than 20 percent of their original transcript was highlighted.

As a result, they filtered out 80 percent of what they planned to say. The upshot? Every one of them delivered a better message on day two that was more effective AND they were able to do it in three minutes or less.

Mike's new presentation began with this new **grabber opening**, which I define as a different way to begin a presentation to immediately grab your audience's attention:

"Do you know how so many investment salespeople come in and simply want to pitch their latest product? Well, what I do is entirely different. What I want to talk to you about today is what matters most to you and your clients: safety, guarantees, and income."

"To give you some background, my company was founded in 1858. The reason that's important is because we have survived wars, recessions, earthquakes, and depressions, and have kept every promise we have made to our clients. This is an important thing to remember when making an investment that you want to last more than 30 years."

"We have over 5,000 employees worldwide, which is big enough to make us a serious player, but small enough to know who you are."

"Finally, we were recently named one of the best places to work in America. The reason this is important to you is because of the quality and experience of our service representatives, whose average tenure at our company is 12 years. What this means is that a real person will answer your phone call in less than 30 seconds, and they can usually answer your question the first time."

To paraphrase the words of Dorothy Boyd (Renee Zellweger's character from the movie *Jerry Maguire*), Mike had us at hello. Presenting information in this format is radically different from both what he had done in the past and what his audience was anticipating. (They expected Mike to come and make a presentation that was all about his product and himself—and not about what was important to them.)

Mike emailed me a few weeks later. He said after delivering this presentation at a major brokerage firm, he recognized something had changed for the better. Not only had 35 of the 50 audience members requested a one-on-one meeting with him (before, he would have considered three or four a major win), but the manager of this office, who Mike had never been able to see before, asked him to stop by his office before he left for the day. He told Mike that based on what he heard and saw, Mike was welcome in their branch anytime.

Here's the bottom line: The So What Matrix is easy to use when you already possess the So What Mindset. Best of all, the So What Matrix will provide a roadmap to help you prepare your presentations and deliver them consistently. Each time Mike used his So What

Matrix, he was able to review what he had said at his last presentation, as well as make minor adjustments based on the needs of his next audience. It worked for Mike, and it can work for you.

TAKE-AWAY IDEAS

1. **The So What Filter is like polarized lenses.** By helping you see what others might miss, even though it's right in front of their eyes.

2. **Use the So What Matrix to prepare your presentations.**

   ▶ **For What?** For what reason are you giving the presentation?

   ▶ **So What?** Why is this important to my audience?

   ▶ **Now What?** What do you want to have happen as a result of your presentation?

3. **After you write a memo, prepare a speech, or create a PowerPoint presentation,** use a highlighter and strike out everything that does not clarify to your audience what's in it for them.

"WRITE YOUR INJURIES
IN DUST AND
YOUR BENEFITS
IN MARBLE."
—BEN FRANKLIN

CHAPTER 5
WHAT'S IN IT FOR THEM?

Released in 1968, the groundbreaking movie *2001: A Space Odyssey* showed us what life would be like in the twenty-first century. In one scene, Dr. Haywood Floyd, who is aboard the Aries Shuttle, wants to contact the Clavius Moon Colony to speak with his family. He does what any space father from the future would do. He uses the phone to call home. Floyd rings from a hands-free videophone with a 20" display that even takes credit cards.

In imagining the future, perhaps director Stanley Kubrick, who also wrote the screenplay (along with Arthur C. Clarke), was inspired by the 1964 New York World's Fair, where AT&T first presented its breakthrough in telecommunications: the PicturePhone. Hailed as a technological marvel, the PicturePhone ended up being what can only be described as a failure—but it was not for lack of trying on AT&T's part.

At the time, AT&T was not only the biggest company in the world, but it had enormous research and development capabilities, thanks to its wholly owned subsidiaries, Bell Labs (research) and Western Electric (development/manufacturing). Those two divisions allowed AT&T to create breakthrough products, from the transistor to the touchtone phone, and bring them successfully to market.

The PicturePhone was expected to be no different.

Invented at Bell Labs in 1956, AT&T subjected it to eight years of tests and improvements before it was released in 1964. "Someday you will be a star" was one of the advertising slogans it used to promote this high-tech and futuristic communications device.[1]

The pitch was simple: Imagine seeing the person you are calling at the same time you are hearing his/her voice.

Figuring that people have the same desire to make eye contact on the phone as they do in person, AT&T marketed this benefit as the primary reason to have a PicturePhone, downplaying the fact that it would cost $125 a month to rent the phones from Western Electric and between $16 and $27 for a three-minute call.[2]

AT&T executives expected five million PicturePhones to be in use by the mid-1980s and to be generating $5 billion in new revenue from this product.

---

[1] Visit sowhatbook.com for further pictures and details.

[2] If that sounds like a lot, it is. Adjusting for inflation, this would be between $107 and $180 for a three-minute call today.

By 1973, after having invested more than a billion dollars, AT&T acknowledged that the PicturePhone was not commercially viable and ended the project less than a decade after heralding this breakthrough in communication.[3]

When reading the post-mortems of what happened, some will tell you the PicturePhone failed because of the small screen size and granular picture, which was the result of the limited bandwidth of the network. Others say it was because of the high cost. I believe both these explanations are incorrect.

More than 40 years after *2001: A Space Odyssey* was released, I can use one of the simplest video-conferencing features ever created, iChat, on my Apple computer. It enables me to see a full-screen picture in decent resolution for free over the Internet—and yet I rarely use this feature. The only time I do is to see my children or have them show me something, such as a drawing or Lego spaceship they have created, while I'm traveling.

Otherwise, the same problem that existed in 1964 is still present today. In most cases, I do not need

---

[3] By 1992, AT&T teed up the idea again as part of their phone system, and once again, it failed to catch on.

to see the person to whom I am speaking, nor am I interested in having him or her see me. The fact is after the "wow" factor wears off, most people will admit that answering the phone first thing in the morning or late at night (or even while you are at work) and having the person be able to see you is not something that people care enough to pay for.

If AT&T executives had understood the real **So What Benefit** of the telephone—the ability to connect with anyone, anywhere, anytime—they might have invested more time and energy in developing new voice technologies, like the cell phone, instead of wasting $1 billion on the PicturePhone.

Let's contrast the failure of the PicturePhone with another revolutionary technology, the iPod, where the outcome has been different.

Thomas Edison invented vinyl records in 1877, and they dominated the way music was recorded and distributed for the next 100 years. In fact, in 1983, some 209 million vinyl long playing (LP) records were sold.

By 1993, this number had declined to 1.2 million: **a 99.5% drop in ten years.**

How could this once-great industry implode so quickly? Because of the introduction of compact discs (CDs). Their So What Benefit was that they were portable, scratch-resistant, and offered incredibly clear digital sound.

Initially, many executives in the vinyl record industry believed that even with those benefits, there was still not much to be worried about, because there was no way the majority of record owners would ever forsake their beloved vinyl records.

These executives were wrong.

Millions of record owners not only made the switch, but they even repurchased many of the same CD albums that they already owned on vinyl records.

Introduced in 1983, the CD became the dominant form of music distribution worldwide by 1995 because the So What Benefit it offered was still relevant.

However, there was another disruptive technology looming on the horizon for the music industry: MP3 files, which could be played on a portable music player.

The CD industry proved to be as clueless as its LP counterparts. They responded by saying in effect, "Why would you need portability when you already have it with a (portable) CD player?" Steve Jobs, CEO of Apple, answered that question with the So What Benefit of the iPod: 1,000 songs in your pocket!

The iPod revolutionized the music industry again, not because people wanted to carry a portable disc drive, but because they loved the idea of carrying 1,000 songs of their choosing with them.

In April 2008, the iTunes Music Store—which is connected to Apple's website and only exists virtually—surpassed Wal-Mart as the largest distributor of music in the United States.

It took more than a decade for CDs to dislodge records; the iPod went from introduction to market leader in just seven years.

What can we learn from these stories?

The PicturePhone lacked a compelling So What Benefit. Remember, a So What Benefit is defined as the benefit that is most important to your audience. The idea that you could see the person you were talking to was a neat feature, but not one that would cause people to go rushing out to get a PicturePhone.

In contrast, the moment people learned that they could carry around 1,000 of their favorite songs on an iPod, millions said, "I love it," "I need it," and "I'll buy it."

WHAT IS YOUR MOMENT?

Think of a typical movie preview. How often has it ended and you've looked to that person sitting with you and said, "I don't think so!," or "We should see it." What is the benefit in your product or service that is going to trigger your audience to say, "I love it," "I need it," and "I'll buy it"?

If you can't think of a So What Benefit, ask a member of your target audience to complete the following sentence:[4]

All I *really* care about is _____.

You may find that they say only one thing, or they may start with one thing and then add two or three

---

[4] I know you are thinking, "I can't ask them to do that," but actually you can. Try saying the following to one of your existing customers, "One of the things that I have found that is really helpful in prioritizing what's most important is to ask you to complete the following sentence regarding this product/service."

more. In either case, generally speaking, what they say first is the So What Benefit you can focus on. If you are just starting up or are looking to discover the So What Benefit for a new product, try out the various benefits on a representative sample of your target audience.

People usually tell themselves a story about why they buy something, and that story can be colored by what they think is culturally acceptable. Those stories are what I call the ***ostensible benefit***—something that might appear true, but is not necessarily the case.

Deep down, emotion almost always trumps the logic when making a buying decision. Finding the So What Benefit helps you connect to that emotion.

Take a look at the following table to better understand the difference between the ostensible benefit and the So What Benefit.

	Ostensible Benefit	So What Benefit
iPod	Portability	1,000 songs of your choice in your pocket
Blackberry	Send and receive email	Stay connected
Microwave	Cook fast	Save time
Your product/ service here	*The benefit that seems like the reason people buy your product*	*The benefit that causes them to say, "I love it, I want it, I'll buy it"*

Here's an example to show how the difference between the ostensible benefit and the So What Benefit would play in practice.

A friend of mine was shopping for a new car, and the one she was considering was the Toyota Prius.

Upon arrival at the dealership, the salesperson focused on the fact that the Prius would help her reduce emissions and thereby help the global warming movement.

This is a great example of the routine/boring/dull/ostensible/unimaginative thinking you can fall into if you don't understand the difference between the ostensible benefit and the So What Benefit.

The fact is that people buy things because of what's in it for them, not you. Although it is undoubtedly true for some people that the So What Benefit when it comes to buying a car is how environmentally friendly it is, not everyone buys a hybrid car for that reason.

Indeed, my friend liked the idea of a hybrid helping the environment, but what created the "I love it, I want it, I'll buy it" moment for her was the Prius gas mileage. Its superior miles per gallon (mpg) would enable her to not only save money on gas, but also save time.

Her previous car, an SUV, required two to three tanks of gas per week, plus the time to go to the gas station and pump the gas, which she did not enjoy doing.

With the Prius, she not only saves money, because she gets almost 47 miles per gallon compared to the 14 miles per gallon with her SUV, but she also avoids two trips to the gas station every week. She now only has to go once a week, as opposed to three. My friend figures that it saves her conservatively 15 minutes a week, which works out to be 13 hours a year to use for things that are more important to her.

Let me demonstrate the Prius example in the format of the previous table.

	Ostensible Benefit	So What Benefit
Toyota Prius	Better for the environment	Save money and time

The bottom line is we all need to remember that although an ostensible benefit might be obvious, it might not be the one that triggers the moment when your customers decide to say yes.

We also need to remember that there might also be more than one benefit for your respective target markets.

For example, with the Toyota Prius, for some people, it was gas mileage/saving money and time; for others, it was the eco-friendly cache; and for still others, it was the dependability of the Toyota brand. It's always important to find out what benefit(s) matter most to your prospective audience/customers.

Although many people have been trained regarding the importance of conducting a "needs analysis" of their audience, the fact is that the majority of salespeople don't do it effectively or consistently. That said, determining the most important benefit to your audience could help you be in the 20 percent who make 80 percent of all sales.

So, how do you do figure out what the So What Benefit is? In my experience, there is usually one benefit that is disproportionately important to the people who you are asking to make a decision.

Let's review how the car salesperson, Phil, could change his approach to understand what mattered to his prospect, Annie, before he began his sales pitch.

Imagine if he had said the following:

> *Phil:* Annie, whenever I meet someone for the first time, I don't ever want to take for granted that I know what's most important to you in purchasing a new car. I'd like to ask you a few questions to find out what's most important to you before we talk about a specific make and model. Is that okay?
>
> *Annie:* Sure.
>
> *Phil:* What are you hoping to accomplish with the purchase of car?
>
> *Annie:* I just want to spend less money on gas and have a reliable car.
>
> *Phil:* Okay. Let me ask you one more question to help prioritize your needs. In terms of why you are buying this car, how would you complete this sentence: "All I really care about is _____."
>
> *Annie:* Hmmm…. All I really care about is spending less money on gas.

Although this dialogue might be oversimplified based on your world, the principle is the same. Namely, it helps you quickly establish the answer to the question, "All I really care about is …" and demonstrate that you are in a different league from most of your competition, who begin selling a benefit that is important to them—or the one that they *assume* will be a benefit to customers—rather than finding out the benefit that's important to their audience.

If you are testing an idea for a marketing piece, you can use this same approach with your survey audience. You can try different copy and headlines for direct response mailing or Internet advertising to see which one generates the best response from your target audience. Sometimes, changing one word or one sentence in an advertisement, marketing piece, or even script that your salespeople use can increase its effectiveness dramatically.

If you make a pie chart and assign relative percentages to the key benefits of your product or service—based on what your audience has told you—invariably it will often become self-evident which one you should lead with in a specific situation.

In the next chapter, "Who You Always Wanted to Be—Yourself," you will see how a **So What Communicator** ties together the everything you've learned so far while remaining authentic.

TAKE-AWAY IDEAS

1. Not all benefits are created equal; to paraphrase author George Orwell, "some benefits are more equal than others." Some benefits help you create a moment that causes your audience to buy. Your job is to ask the right questions to figure out which benefit is most important to your audience.

2. To determine the So What Benefit, use the sentence-completion technique by asking your audience/prospect to complete this statement: "All I really care about is _____."

3. Lead your marketing with the benefit that causes your audience to respond with "I love it," "I need it," and "I'll buy it."

"WHEN I JOINED THE PROFESSIONAL GOLF ASSOCIATION TOUR IN 1967, I WAS A NOBODY. AND WHEN I TOLD MY JOKES, NO ONE LAUGHED. THEN IN 1968, I WON THE U.S. OPEN, AND AFTER THAT WHEN I TOLD THE SAME JOKES, EVERYONE LAUGHED LIKE HELL."
—LEE TREVINO

CHAPTER 6
WHO YOU ALWAYS WANTED TO BE—YOURSELF

Lee Trevino can afford to laugh. In the world of professional golf, his swing has been the subject of many discussions—almost none of them flattering. He developed his now-famous inside-out swing as he taught himself to play golf.

Even so, Trevino won 29 times on the PGA Tour, including six majors, and he was named Sportsman of the Year by *Sports Illustrated*. I often use Lee Trevino as an example of authenticity in my role as a presentation coach. I say to my students, "Can you imagine if a golf coach had come up to Lee Trevino and said, 'I work with Jack Nicklaus (the Tiger Woods of his day), and I'd like to show you how to transform your golf swing to make it more like Jack's.'"

Chances are Trevino would have said he didn't want to be like Jack Nicklaus. He wanted to be like Lee Trevino.

Why are we talking about Lee Trevino?

One of the foundational principles of applying the **So What Mindset** in a presentation—whether it is one-to-one, talking to a small group, or speaking to a large audience—is remaining authentic to who you are. Everything begins with that. If you are trying to be someone you are not, people will catch on, and they will spend all their time thinking about how phony you are instead of about what you are saying.

But just because you are going to be authentic doesn't mean you can't use some help when it comes to presenting your message. That's what this chapter is about. In order to understand what is different about someone who employs a So What Mindset in all his communication (let's call him a So What Communicator for simplicity's sake), you need to think about the three stages—the before, during, and after—of any communication.

The first distinction between So What Communicators and everyone else is that they think about these three stages long before they get in front of an audience.

Let me tell you about one of my first coaching assignments that provided me with a breakthrough in my thinking as a result of helping my client, Neil.

Unfortunately, for Neil, it was over before it began.

Armed with 60 sandwiches and soft drinks, plus the brochures explaining the financial product he was selling, Neil arrived at the mahogany-paneled boardroom of a large Boston brokerage firm to deliver a lunchtime presentation.

Neil had hired me to observe his presentation and give him some pointers on how he could be more effective as a presenter.

I sat in the back and watched people walk into the conference room, collect a sandwich and a drink, and immediately walk back out. They had no intention of attending the presentation. But they were happy to help themselves to a free lunch.

Neil looked on helplessly as within just ten minutes, the mountain of food he had brought was whittled down to just two sandwiches—and yet there were only nine people sitting in the room that had been set up to accommodate 50.

He didn't help things with his opening line: "It's okay to keep eating while I am speaking because I know how valuable your time is."

That forced him to speak over the sounds of sandwiches being unwrapped and soft drinks opened, which could explain why it sounded at times as if Neil was yelling as he talked about his financial products.

It was clear, from my vantage point, that his presentation held no interest to the nine people present. In fact, five minutes into the presentation,

Neil had lost the group to such an extent that several of them started reading the *Wall Street Journal*!

The net effect of all this was like watching a car accident in slow motion. It provided a flashback to my traumatic experience with Jeff Goldberg the day I had to deliver my presentation to an audience of one—him.

Neil ended his presentation with a desperate plea for the handful of people there to buy his product. Less than ten seconds after he said, "Thank you for your time," the audience had escaped, and it was just Neil and those two (now slightly wilted) sandwiches in the room.

Neil began a slow trek toward where I was sitting, and I knew what was coming.

"So, what did you think?"

I paused because I know how fragile we all are when we put ourselves out "in the arena," and how hard it is to accept constructive criticism and coaching with an open mind. I chose my words carefully and said, "I am surprised by the level of disrespect you've received from this audience."

Neil's face went blank, and then I saw a flash of anger. He said, "See. I told you. These people are idiots, and they don't value what I do."

I said, "I understand how you feel, and I have some disturbing news. I don't think it's their fault."

"Are you saying it's my fault?"

I simply looked at him.

He said, "How is that possible? I showed up early. I brought food and drinks. I practiced my presentation. I told them everything I thought they needed to hear about my products, and I even ended early. How could this be my fault?"

I said, "Neil, here's the simple reality. This game was over before it began. This audience made up their mind that it was not useful to listen to you even before you started talking. Let me tell you why."

"This audience doesn't know you the way I do. They don't know that you served in the United States Air Force. They don't know that you are a world-class marathon runner who qualified for the U.S. Olympic Trials. They don't know that you have helped hundreds of people, people just like them, to grow their business using the specific strategies and tools you came to talk about."

"Because they didn't know this, their preconceived idea was that you are like all the rest of 'your kind'— a waste of their time."

"Think about a farmer who is about to sow his field. Would he just throw the seeds on dry dirt? Of course not. He would till the soil, so that the seeds could easily take hold. What you just did was throw seed on dry, unprepared soil."

"I can show you how to prepare the soil so that your seeds, your ideas, will not only germinate but will produce results that are twenty, fifty, or even a hundred times what you expected. In your case, that means more well-qualified prospects."

Neil said, "How are we going to do that?"

"We are going to position you like we would any other product: By understanding what's important to your audience and then focusing on those benefits that are relevant to them."

We headed off for coffee and began planning Neil's next presentation, which I promised him would go far better. To help give him the appropriate frame of reference, I told him about a recent trip I took to Disney World with my family. Walt Disney was a master at setting the stage for his audience, and I told Neil that we could harness the power of this approach as well.

For example, you don't just get out of your car and walk up to the front door of Cinderella's castle at Disney World. Instead, your experience begins the moment you enter the parking area and get on a monorail, tram, or paddleboat that takes you into the park. On the way in, you will see shrubbery that has been carved into the shape of various Disney characters, and if you pass one of the golf courses, you realize that the sand traps are shaped like Mickey Mouse's head.

But soon enough, as you draw closer, you will spot, as my son did, the peak of Cinderella's castle drawing nearer. "There it is!," he shouted. As the monorail pulled into the station, there was a palpable excitement level that was completely different than if we had simply parked our car and walked into the theme park. I told Neil we would set the stage for him just like Walt Disney did for his guests.

After we ordered our coffees, I asked Neil several questions. The first was, "How much do you know about the people you expect to attend your next presentation?"

"Well, I've been to their office three times before and I know a few of them."

I asked, "Do you know who the key decision makers are or the centers of influence?"

"Not really."

I then asked him, "Would it be helpful to understand what key concerns your audience has, especially as they relate to your products?" He replied, "Of course."

Because he was selling investment products to financial advisors who would recommend them to their clients, one of the primary concerns his audience had was the long-term performance and track record of his products and how they fared in bear as well as bull markets. He agreed that it would be extremely beneficial to address these concerns, since it would help him tailor his presentation, but he wasn't sure where to begin.

BEFORE THE PRESENTATION

I showed Neil just how easy it was to get that kind of information before his presentation. In fact, I demonstrated one example for him while we were having coffee. I "Googled" the manager of the office where Neil had just completed his presentation, and it gave us 10 solid hits—everything from a copy of his personal biography (which was attached to a speech he had given recently) to an industry paper in which he was quoted discussing asset allocation strategies for a bear market. This was a great tie-in to the types of investment products Neil was offering.

I told Neil he could get similar information on just about everyone else who was important in the company and was likely to be in attendance at his next presentation. That would make it substantially easier to customize his talk. He was unaware of how easy this was to do. A few keystrokes of his own later, and he was convinced.

Next, I asked how he would feel about using a **personal biography**. I explained that this is a written document that communicates the information that most people want to know about you—but are uncomfortable asking about—before they agree to work with you. A personal biography is NOT the same as a business card or a resume. Neil told me that he didn't have anything good to write in a personal biography, and no one in his industry used such a document. I listened to his objections and said, "Would you be willing to try this if I help you create one?"

"I am willing to try anything to keep from going through a presentation like the one you just witnessed," he responded.

I told Neil that a personal biography was not a new idea. In fact, almost everyone who is an executive, doctor, professor, movie star, author, or otherwise considered to be an "important person" has a personal biography. I suggested that Neil look at his own company's website that had brief biographies on the CEO and the entire management team. The format I was suggesting to Neil was a variation of the type of biography that other "important people" use because it included what he could do for his clients.

It's an idea that was discussed in the book by Napoleon Hill, *Think and Grow Rich*, in the 1930s to help people differentiate themselves during the Great Depression. Hill said a personal biography "is not a tool of clever salesmanship by which men and women demand and receive more money for the same services they formerly sold for less pay. Rather it's about the interests of the purchaser as well as the seller of personal services to ensure the employer receives full value for the additional value he pays."

In essence, Napoleon Hill explained how this tool helped people earn more money even during a difficult economic time by communicating the real value they delivered.

Lastly, I asked Neil how often he had someone introduce him before he started speaking. He said he had asked someone to introduce him in the past, but gave up on it because of how poorly it was delivered. Besides, in the case of the upcoming speech, he thought enough people knew who he was to make a formal introduction unnecessary.

I made a few notes as Neil talked and said, "I want to help you make this work, but in order for us to move forward, you have to be willing to trust me and try what I recommend, exactly the way I show you. I do not want to be debating with you on each step regarding the efficacy of these ideas."

As we finished our coffee, Neil agreed that for his next presentation, he would follow my prescription to the letter.

The first thing I did was help Neil create his own personal biography (and I urge you to do the same thing). In short, it is a brief overview of the following:

▶ Who you are.

▶ Your character, competence, and common ground (educational background, fraternal organizations, hobbies, home town, sports interests, and so on).

▶ What makes you unique.

But, you cannot construct it in a vacuum. Like everything else you do, your personal biography needs to be created with the So What Filter clearly in mind. In other words, everything you write must be relevent to the audience who is going to read it. For example, you want to be sure to talk about what you can do for them and avoid jargon and acronyms that people might not understand.

In other words, although the biography is about you, it's really about what you do for your clients, customers, and anyone else who is reading it. In short, it is the BENEFIT you bring to the table for them that will solve *their* problem, answer *their* questions, or eliminate *their* pain.

How do you create such a biography?[1] Here are the steps:

1. Complete the 10 questions on the Personal Biography Generator.

2. Using the answers on the Personal Biography Generator, draft your biography in such a way that it is clear, compelling, and relevant.

---

[1] See sowhatbook.com for biography examples.

3. Triple check to see that everything is not only consistent but also accurate. Failure to do so can be career ending. For example, attending a continuing education class at Harvard is not the same as graduating from Harvard University.

4. Use a graphic designer to lay out the final copy to make it as visually appealing as possible. You can use a standard 8 ½" × 11" size or consider trying a different layout that helps your biography stand out—for example, 8 ½" × 5 ½". If necessary, be sure to have your compliance or legal department sign off on your biography before printing.

5. Print color copies of your biography on thick card stock for distribution as part of your new client or customer kit. You will also want to post it on your website.

6. Make sure to present your personal biography prior to meeting people, whether one-on-one or in groups, for the first time. It's normal to feel awkward when doing this, if you think the biography is all about you. But it really isn't. Your personal biography is not meant to "blow your own horn," but rather help the other person better understand what you can do for them WITHOUT you spending so much time talking about your company or about yourself once you finally meet.

7. Update your biography at least once a year in order to include any relevant changes.

Neil took a very different approach to his next talk. For one thing, he called the office manager and asked if he would be willing to introduce him to the group as part of his preparation before the presentation.

The office manager, Bill, said he would be glad to. He asked Neil what he wanted him to say to the group. In the past, when Neil had asked someone to introduce him—which he rarely did—Neil had made a tactical error by allowing the person doing the introduction to "wing it," using Neil's business card or perhaps some collateral material Neil had sent, as the basis of his script.

Neil sent Bill the *exact* text he wanted him to read and explained that it was designed specifically for this group and was meant to be read, not memorized.

By telling him this, Neil was doing two subtle things.

First, he was underscoring that Bill wouldn't have to do anything hard as part of the introduction.

Second, it increased the chances that Bill would actually read as written what Neil had sent.

Here's what the introduction said:

Introduction Card—Neil Wood

Today, we are fortunate to have with us an expert on the topic of creating a stream of income your clients can't outlive.

Neil brings a unique combination of success, both as a professional athlete and as a presenter within the investment industry.

Neil understands the opportunities and challenges we face and has created a presentation that has been customized for our office called "Making Your Money Last a Lifetime."

Please join me in welcoming Neil Wood.

DURING THE PRESENTATION

Next, he used the So What Matrix you learned about in Chapter 4, "Your World View—Making the Invisible Visible," to make sure his presentation passed the **So What Test**—the internal dialogue he had with himself to determine whether his message mattered to his audience.

When we arrived the day of the presentation, we stopped by Bill's office at 11:30 a.m. in plenty of time for the noon start time.

Neil was fearful that the same thing that happened last time would happen again. But it didn't. At our suggestion, Bill had sent out an email the day before, telling everyone that Neil would be coming. And shortly before noon, Bill got on the public address system and reminded the entire office that his friend, Neil Wood, would be delivering a lunch presentation that they wouldn't want to miss.

At 11:55 a.m., people began to stream into the conference room and began collecting the sandwiches off the cart. This time, however, as they sat down, they noticed Neil's personal biography that I had put out on the table in front of each chair, over Neil's protest.

Almost all the seats were filled when Bill stood up. He said, "Before we get started, although some of you already know him, I want to take this opportunity to formally introduce Neil Wood to you." He then read the script Neil had provided to him that ended with, "Please join me in welcoming Neil Wood."

The group applauded Neil as he walked up, and he flashed me a smile because he had never experienced anything like this before. As he began his presentation, I noticed people putting their drinks and sandwiches down as they actually focused on what he was saying. He did not give the audience permission to eat while he spoke, although many did so discreetly.

Neil made the points that were relevant to his audience and ended with a clear call to action based on his original objectives from his So What Matrix and then said:

> If what you heard today makes sense and you want to learn more about how to apply this idea in your business, fill out the profile card on the table in front of you, and you can hand it in to me on your way out. I will be standing over by the door. I'll treat this card as an invitation from you to me to schedule a time to meet with you one-to-one.

Neil delivered those lines with a sense of confidence and conviction and walked off the stage to a round of spirited applause. I could tell from my vantage point that the audience appreciated how different this entire experience was compared to the typical, everyday lunch meeting they were used to enduring.

As Neil stood by the door, I saw person after person hand him the card and then make a comment about his talk, or ask him a question based on something they read on his personal biography.

When the last audience member finally left, Neil walked over and said, "Okay. I guess this works."

Out of 47 people who had attended the meeting, he received 35 profile cards. This 75 percent response rate was an all-time record for him, based on his typical results of only 0 to 20 percent requesting a meeting.

AFTER THE PRESENTATION

In following up with those 37 people, Neil took a short time not only to study the card they had given him, but also to do a bit of research so that his follow-up letter and phone call would be as effective as possible.

Neil generated 26 one-to-one meetings, and over the next 90 days, he ended up doing business with 18 members of the original audience. Unlike the past, the return-on-investment for the cost of his lunch meeting was now an exponential return.

Neil had to change his thinking to apply these ideas and become a So What Communicator; however, to be authentic, he had to tailor this process to make it work for him. If this process were easy, everyone would do it. It's not, and so they don't. Neil applied this process to separate himself from the crowd and transform the results he achieved. You can, too.

TAKE-AWAY IDEAS

1. **Before, during, and after….** What you do before and after your presentation may be as important as what you do during your presentation.

2. Remain authentic to yourself and connect with your audience. If you try to be someone you are not, people will catch on, and they will spend all their time thinking about how phony you are instead of thinking about what you are saying.

3. The So What Communicator uses this process to maximize the return on time invested.

"I SKATE TO WHERE THE PUCK IS GOING TO BE."
—WAYNE GRETZKY

CHAPTER 7
WINGING IT VERSUS ORCHESTRATION

It was a cold day in Geneva, Switzerland in 1985 when Ronald Reagan did something that helped create his nickname "The Great Communicator." He was meeting Soviet Premier Mikhail Gorbachev to discuss a potential reduction in the arsenals of the United States and the Soviet Union. The meeting was the first attempt to create a thaw in the Cold War since Gorbachev had come into power.

Because of his life experience and knowledge of what had happened under the leadership of the Communist party, President Reagan had, prior to the meeting, repeatedly referred to the Soviet Union as an "evil empire."

Premier Gorbachev had basically the same views of the United States, having been taught about the corrupting influences of a consumer society and how the Communist party believed the United States government secretly desired to dominate the whole world—including the Soviet Union.

When the subject of arms negotiations came up during their meeting, President Reagan did something that surprised everyone in the room. He turned to Mr. Gorbachev and said, "Why don't you and I go for a short walk and get some fresh air, and let the rest of our people talk about some of the details regarding a potential arms treaty?"

Mr. Gorbachev immediately got out of his seat, even as his diplomats expressed surprise about this seemingly impromptu change in the formal agenda.

In an interview later, President Reagan revealed what happened next. He escorted Premier Gorbachev to a lakeside cottage, where there was already a fire burning.

As they sat alone before the fire, President Reagan said, "We don't mistrust each other because we are armed; we are armed because we mistrust each other. While it's all right for us to talk about reducing the number of warheads we have, why don't you and I see if we can eliminate the things that cause the mistrust?"

His point being, of course, that if both countries truly trusted each other, they would be able to significantly reduce their nuclear arsenals.

The rest of the conversation that took place that afternoon was simply designed for the two world leaders to get to know one another.

On the way back to the general meeting after their hour and a half together at the cottage, President Reagan said, "Why don't we agree that next year, the summit will be in the United States?"

"I accept," said Mr. Gorbachev, who added, "then the following year, the summit will be in Moscow."

President Reagan said, "I accept."

Ronald Reagan's action to change the political dialogue between these super powers was the beginning of the end of the Cold War. His preparation, orchestration, and delivery of the right words at the right time helped make this possible.

WHAT WENT ON HERE

Do you think it was a coincidence that the cottage where Reagan and Gorbachev met privately was only a short distance from the main house and that the fire was burning and the lights were on when they walked in?

Obviously not.

In his exchange with Gorbachev, President Reagan employed the idea of the So What Matrix and a sequence of questions or bullet points that helped him anticipate what mattered most to Mr. Gorbachev and collect the information he needed to know what to do next.

Using the idea of the So What Matrix discussed in Chapter 4, "Your World View—Making the Invisible Visible," let's take a look at how President Reagan might have filled out the So What Matrix to accomplish his goals:

1. **For What?**

   Q: For what reason am I meeting with Premier Gorbachev?

   A: To determine whether or not he is someone to be trusted and with whom I can have a meaningful arms reduction.

2. **So What?**

   Q: The reason this is important to Premier Gorbachev is because...

   A: His economy cannot sustain the massive spending required to keep up with the technological advances of the United States, which puts his country at risk.

3. **Now What?**

   Q: What do I (President Reagan) want to have happen as a result of this meeting?

   A: Meaningful arms reduction, and a scheduled summit in Washington, D.C.

President Reagan said later, "I told my people in advance that I was going to do something like I did. When we left the building, I made it sound like it was all impromptu."

Before he went to Geneva, as part of his pre-meeting planning, Reagan not only orchestrated his questions but also the location and environment to achieve the desired outcome.

Webster's Dictionary defines "**orchestrate**" as follows: *To organize a situation or an event unobtrusively so that a desired effect or outcome is achieved.*

The opposite of orchestration is what most people do. They "**wing it**." It's a theatrical term meaning to learn your lines just before you go on stage. Reagan, a former actor, demonstrated that the meeting in Geneva was far too important to just "wing it."

When you interact with a prospect, or someone you are hoping to connect with, are you more likely to orchestrate what you want to have happen or do you wing it?

If you want to harness the power of orchestration in your world, here is an idea that can help you. I borrowed the idea from the television program *CSI*, where crime scene investigators often use a very small piece of evidence to determine "who done it."

In much the same way, one small piece of information (from a search on Google, Facebook, and so on) about your audience can help you create the right questions to ask so that you can begin to understand what matters to them.

Reagan utilized his own version of "CSI research" in the form of an intelligence briefing about the Soviet Union to better understand the So What Benefit he could offer Gorbachev so that he, in turn, could get what he wanted—a meaningful arms reduction.

30,000 FEET VERSUS SEA LEVEL

Ronald Reagan understood the difference between asking questions at a **30,000-foot level versus sea level**. In the same way, certain questions have a big picture viewpoint as if you are looking at the subject from high in the air.

In order for President Reagan to anticipate the So What Benefit of a meaningful arms reduction for both countries, he had to begin with a 30,000-foot question, "Why don't you and I see if we can eliminate the things that cause the mistrust?" Reagan understood that until he knew whether or not the mistrust between the two countries could be eliminated, it was pointless to think about reducing nuclear arms.

Great communicators often start their questioning process at the big picture 30,000-foot strategic level and then come down to sea level as they understand more about the So What Benefit to their audience.

Too often, salespeople—which includes anyone selling anything, whether it is a product, service, or an idea (so, it's all of us)—have a tendency to begin at sea level with tactical questions specific to the product, service, or idea they are selling. If Reagan had begun their summit meeting by saying, "I am willing to cut 100 missiles in West Germany if you are willing to cut 100 in East Germany," he never would have gotten to the real issue.

This is not to say that tactical questions and sea-level viewpoints are never necessary. When what you are selling is of a "transactional" nature, it might make sense to begin at sea level to complete the transaction. A cashier at a supermarket typically does not need to begin at the 30,000-foot level, but rather can engage you at sea level with, "Will that be cash or credit?"

Here's a typical example of starting with sea-level questioning. Recently, I went to buy a new personal computer for my family. Here is a verbatim account of what happened:

Salesperson: Can I help you?

Mark: I'm looking for a computer for my family.

Salesperson: How much are you looking to spend?

Mark: I'm not really sure. How much are they?

Salesperson: Between $500 and $5000.

Mark: Under $1000.

Salesperson: How many gigabytes do you need?

Mark: I have no idea.

Salesperson: What speed processor are you looking for?

Mark: I really don't know.

> Salesperson: What do you want to do with
> this computer?
>
> Mark: That's easy. I want to surf the Internet,
> check email, and download music.
>
> Salesperson: Okay, then you need to look over
> here at our "Family Edition Media Computer,"
> and in fact, it's on sale....

Notice what happened here. The salesperson started
at sea level, and only at the point where I was feeling
frustrated did he finally jump up to a 30,000-foot
more strategic question, which was, "What do you
want to do with this computer?"

He eventually got to where he needed to go, but not
before he made the customer (me) feel like an idiot,
which is never a good sales strategy.

Now, let's look at what would have happened if he had
started in the right place, which in this case means at
30,000 feet:

> Salesperson: Can I help you?
>
> Mark: I'm looking for a computer for my
> family.

Salesperson: What would you like to do with this computer?

Mark: That's easy. I want to surf the Internet, check email, and download music.

Salesperson: Okay. Now, to help me better understand which computer to recommend, I need to know if you plan to store digital photographs on your computer in addition to your music?

Mark: Yes.

Salesperson: Okay, then what I would suggest for your family is our "Family Edition Media Computer" because it is designed for people who want to do the three things you mentioned and enable each family member to have their own section so that they can each keep their own personalized files separate.

Mark: Great.

Salesperson: It happens that this particular computer is on sale…and we have a service plan for $79.00 where we can deliver the computer, set it up, and get everything running for you.

Mark: Terrific. Let's do it. Here's my credit card.

What this dialogue demonstrates is that the way you sequence your questions can fundamentally alter the experience of your audience and move them to the "I love it, I need it, I'll buy it" moment. Do it right, and they will understand the So What Benefit of what you are selling, and the point you are trying to make.

Let's look at another fairly typical sales situation:

> Scenario: You are calling on a new prospect and want to get to the So What Benefit before pitching your product/service.

> You (*ask the 30,000-foot question*): What is the biggest opportunity you see to grow your business this year?

> Prospect: The Internet.

> You (*move down to the 20,000-foot question*): What have you done in the past to grow your business on the Internet?

> Prospect: Not much. We just have a website, but do not sell anything online.

> You (*now the 10,000-foot question*): Which products would you like to sell on the Internet?

> Prospect: Our widget.

You (*ask the sea-level question*): Based
on what you've said, I have a few ideas
that I would like to share with you. Is this
something you would like to talk about now
or the next time we meet?

Odds are they are going to say, "Can we talk about
it now?"

Anticipating the So What Benefit does require a bit
of work. You need to think through all the things that
might happen in your interaction with your audience.
But that's okay. The payoff is worth it.

That's a lesson Ronald Reagan learned early in his
political life. A So What Communicator needs to think
about and orchestrate in advance the questions he is
going to ask to accomplish his desired outcome. You
should do no less.

Every day, good people fail because they "wing
it" rather than invest a little time and attention in
orchestrating the right questions to ask before they
start to speak. Just like The Great Gretzky focused on
where the puck was going rather than where it was,
you need to think about where your communication
is going and not just where it is.

TAKE-AWAY IDEAS

1. Prepare by doing your version of "CSI research." Use the Internet or your own "intelligence network" to understand more about your customers and clients before you open your mouth.

2. Start at 30,000 feet versus sea level with the questions you ask. Look at the big picture before you engage "tactically" at sea level.

3. Orchestrate versus winging it. Using the So What Matrix, plan the flow of your conversation to get to the "I love it, I need it, I'll buy it" moment.

"THE DIFFERENCE
BETWEEN THE RIGHT
WORD AND ALMOST
THE RIGHT WORD
IS THE DIFFERENCE
BETWEEN LIGHTNING
AND A LIGHTNING
BUG."
—MARK TWAIN

CHAPTER 8
GETTING YOUR AUDIENCE
ENGAGED

Most people feel anxious when they're asked: "What business are you in?" That is perfectly understandable.

The fact is the cliché, "You never get a second chance to make a first impression," is absolutely right. And the way you answer the question, "What do you do for a living?" usually determines whether or not people will want to listen to what you have to say.

That's why you want to get your audience engaged immediately. You do that through creating a **So What Positioning Statement**, which is designed to cause your listener to want to know more about you and what you can do for them. To be effective, your So What Positioning Statement must be clear, compelling, and relevant to your listener.

Unfortunately, very few of us can do this without some help. I learned that lesson several years ago when I was presenting a series of marketing seminars to small-business owners who were customers of Staples.

During the three years I did the seminars, I had the opportunity to meet more than 3,000 entrepreneurs, men and women who represented almost every imaginable industry—from landscape architects to funeral directors; from ambulance service operators to real estate agents.

I began each seminar by asking people their names and what business they were in.

Inevitably, they would only mention the commodity aspect of what they did. They would say something like: "My name is John, and I sell computers." Or "My name is Jane, and I am in the real estate business."

Almost no one communicated the real So What Benefit they offered, or any unique aspects about themselves or what they did.

However, Floyd's response to "tell everyone what you do for a living" was not typical. After giving his name, he said he was "an automotive consultant."

I was unsure what he meant, so I asked him if he was a consultant to the major auto manufacturers.

"*No.*"

"Do you consult to the local franchises?"

"*No.*"

Somewhat exasperated, I finally asked, "What do you *really* do?"

Floyd said, "Do you know how so many people don't like the process of buying a new car because they don't like dealing with the salesperson?

I said, "Yes."

"Well, what I do, for $295, is take people through a 15-point process designed to help them determine the exact right car for them, and then I go with them to the dealership to negotiate the best price."

As soon as he finished speaking, there was an electrical charge in the room. It was as if everyone knew that Floyd did something unique. In fact, I noticed the woman sitting behind Floyd reach up and tap him on the shoulder to ask for his business card.

All through the rest of the seminar, I kept wondering if other people would remember Floyd's positioning statement in the same way I did. So, just before the seminar ended, I asked a participant I chose at random if she remembered what business Floyd was in.

She said, "Oh, sure. For $295, he takes you through a 15-point process to help you determine the best car for you to buy and then he goes with you to the dealership to help you buy it."

This was an "Aha!" moment for me. Not only did she understand what Floyd had said, but also more importantly she was able to repeat it back in her own words, capturing his unique So What Benefit.

Think of the leverage it creates for you and your organization when everyone can communicate the So What Benefit of what you do in such a clear and compelling way that your audience wants to know exactly how you do that.

Floyd had done exactly that.

You can use the formula behind the strategy Floyd employed so effectively as well, no matter what you do for a living.

Let's look at exactly what he did.

The first thing he said was "Do you know how...?" followed with "Well, what I do is...."

Over the years, I have seen this model used successfully in literally hundreds of businesses across multiple industries. There is a great deal of power in using this approach, even though some people might find it to be a little awkward at first. This power comes from having a prepared collection of words that you can deliver authentically, which enables you to focus more on the response from your listener than on worrying about what you are going to say next. It also provides an orchestrated approach to creating curiosity about who you are and what you do.

Although it's easy to think you might come across as "canned" if you prepare what you will say in advance, the alternative is to create the wrong first impression and lose the chance to create the right association to the real value you can deliver because you thought you could wing it.

Try using this model until you have a So What Positioning Statement that causes people to respond, "How do you do that?." That is the litmus test for the success of a So What Positioning Statement. When someone says, "How do you do that?," you know you have struck a chord for something that is important and relevant to them. It's also an invitation for you to tell them more about your product or service—either now or at a later date.

Here is an example of how taking this approach can turn out to be extremely helpful.

A client of mine, Frank, was a top sales performer at his company, but he had always struggled with the right way to position what he really did.

He had been taught that the best way to answer the question, "What do you do?," was to immediately respond with "I sell life insurance!"

That answer, while true, typically produced a look of momentary panic on the faces of his audience, who immediately began to back away from him.

The problem with what he had been taught was that although it might have been accurate, it was all about his product and not about what he did for his clients.

How does the fact that Frank sells life insurance benefit listeners, unless at that moment they happen to be in the market for purchasing life insurance? Instead, they will most likely be thinking, "So what?," and an opportunity will have been lost.

Explaining the So What Positioning Statement to him, coupled with a little bit of coaching, made a huge difference in how he responded to the question, "and what is it that you do?." His answer is now clear, compelling, and relevant to his audience, as you are about to see.

Frank had just arrived at his favorite golf course and was introduced to the other two members of his foursome, both business owners. Before they teed off, one of the business owners asked Frank: "So, what do you do?"

Without missing a beat and appearing spontaneous, Frank said: "Do you know how most business owners have a CFO to help them manage their company's money?"

The business owner said, "Yes." (By this point, the other businessman was listening in as well.)

"Well, what I do is work as a personal CFO for my clients to help them make work optional."

"How do you do that?"

Frank said, "I'll be happy to tell you more about it after the round. For now, let's enjoy the golf."

Inside, Frank was beaming with confidence, knowing he said exactly what he rehearsed while sounding spontaneous and unscripted.

He called me on his way home. "*I can't believe how well this worked.*" He told me what had happened on the golf course, adding, "I have appointments to meet with both of them (individually) next week."

Although Frank's So What Positioning Statement sounds simple, it took us about three hours to create, and that does not include all the time Frank spent rehearsing it. Part of this process included determining Frank's **Ideal Client Profile**. I had Frank describe his top five clients and what he liked most about working with them. He said that what four of them had in common was that they didn't need the money but still worked as if their business depended on it. He continued that they liked the fact that work is optional for them.

From this research, I determined that the words we wanted to use would be designed to resonate best with someone who wanted work to be optional. If you think about your positioning statement like a lure that is designed to catch a certain type of fish, you will understand that a small change can make a huge difference in what type of "fish" you catch. Sometimes you will catch something unanticipated, but what makes this approach unique is consciously directing your attention toward finding your ideal client rather than anyone who might come along.

By understanding that Frank's target market was people who owned businesses who didn't want to fully retire, but wanted work to be optional, we had the So What Benefit that was most important to this type of person.

Frank's So What Positioning Statement landed two outstanding prospects who were eager to continue the conversation.

Now, imagine if Frank had answered the "So, what do you do?" question with "I sell life insurance."

It probably would have ruined their golf game.

IF AT FIRST YOU DON'T SUCCEED

It usually takes at least three revisions of any So What Positioning Statement before you create one that is compelling. Using the structure ("Do you know how…? Well, what I do is….") is the best format I've found to get started.

There is another benefit to using this strategy. It has to do with context and timing.

Some people believe that any direct question ("What do you do?") should only be answered with an immediate direct answer ("I am in sales.").

However, by using this approach, you are given a moment to think and set up what I call **Psychic Real Estate**—the words, pictures, and feelings you want people to associate with you and your product or service. And that pause subconsciously tells your audience that they are not going to hear a typical answer.

By asking the rhetorical question, "Do you know how most people don't like the process of buying a new car, because they don't like dealing with a salesperson?," Floyd used the psychological concept called "the undeniable truth." He was offering a statement that almost everyone believes, and it had the natural effect of causing people to nod their heads in agreement.

Virtually every great communicator, from presidents to entertainers, uses this strategy. Earlier we talked about Ronald Reagan's use of orchestration, but he was also known for using the concept of the undeniable truth in his speeches. For example, during one state of the union, he said, "Our tax code is too complex." and proceeded to pick up a stack of papers more than 12 inches high to visually demonstrate this point. The undeniable truth helps create a context where people are signaling that they are in agreement with you and are willing to listen to what you say next.

This approach paved the way for Floyd to say: "Well, what I do is…."

The simple fact is that fully 50 percent of the time people are not mentally engaged in what you are saying until you grab their attention. The So What Positioning Statement acts like a hook to grab their attention before you deliver your punch line.

Think of the way the news media uses a "hook" both in newspaper and television news to get your attention so that you will want to know the rest of the story. "Orange juice that could kill you...more at 11" would likely get your attention versus "Latest research in *Journal of Microbiology* on citrus-based juices."

If your audience doesn't understand your rhetorical question ("Do you know how...?"), or don't agree with it, then it is unlikely they will understand or respond to whatever you were going to say as the follow-up ("Well, what I do is...."). That's why you need to craft your So What Positioning Statement so carefully.

I encourage you to develop at least two versions of your So What Positioning Statement.

Frank developed a generic version for people he met who were not part of his primary target market (his family, neighbors, someone he met casually) to answer the "So what do you do?" question, and he used it to clarify what he really did. Frank also developed a "primary target market version" for the people who fit his ideal client profile (used in the previous story).

Here are Frank's two positioning statements:[1]

>**Generic version:** Do you know how most people are worried about running out of money at retirement? Well, what I do is help my clients to create a stream of income they can't outlive.

>**Primary target market version:** Do you know how most business owners have a CFO to help them manage their companies' money? Well, what I do is work as a personal CFO for my clients to help them make work optional.

Even if your listener has no need for your product or service, if they can remember what you do, there is a much better chance they will know someone who can benefit from what you do.

After you start using your So What Positioning Statement, you will wonder why it took you so long to start using one.

I received an email from a management consultant named Bob who told me that after completing his So What Positioning Statement in our seminar program,

---

[1] Visit the sowhatbook.com to find a variety of So What Positioning Statements for different services and industries.

he went home and practiced it with his 13-year-old daughter. What he said was, "Do you know how important it is to choose the right words before you tell a friend an important piece of information? Well, what I do is help companies choose the right words to communicate what makes them unique to their customers." She told him it was the first time she ever really understood what he did at work, in spite of the fact that he had tried to explain it to her many times, and he had an MBA. Previously Bob had said, "I help integrate end-to-end, client-focused, value-added communications to empower employees to communicate effectively." It's no wonder his daughter (and just about everyone else who heard the explanation) was confused!

THE SO WHAT POSITIONING STATEMENT GENERATOR

How can you figure out what will be your best So What Positioning Statement? Trying using this approach:

Step 1:   Determine the key issues your clients and
          prospects face.

          Ask the question this way: What are the
          three primary concerns my customers (and
          potential customers) face?

          And then simply list your answers:

          A.

          B.

          C.

Step 2:   What are the three things you do to address
          their primary concerns?

          A.

          B.

          C.

Step 3:   Choose the most relevant of the three
          primary concerns and the best answer from
          step 2 that addresses it.

          Take both, and put it in this format:

          ▶ Do you know how…? (Insert the primary
            concern.)

> ▶ Well, what I do is…. (Insert what you do to
> address the concern.)

Here's an example. Let's say you are a financial advisor:

Step 1:   Determine the key concerns your clients and prospects face.

Their answers might be the following:

A. They are concerned about running out of money in retirement.

B. They are concerned that a catastrophic illness could wipe out their savings.

C. They want to leave some money to their children.

Step 2:   Determine three things that you do to address these primary concerns:

A. Provide guaranteed income.

B. Provide medical insurance.

C. Provide children with tax-free income.

Step 3:   Choose the most relevant of the three
          primary concerns from step 1 and the best
          answer from step 2 that addresses it.

Let's say the client is most concerned about having
enough money to live on in retirement (answer A in
step 1). Clearly, answer A in step 2 is the best fit.

So, you then take answer 1A and 2A and put it into
this format:

> *Do you know how…?* (Insert the primary
> concern.)
>
> *What I do is….* (Insert what you do to address
> the concern.)

If you do, it would sound something like this:

> Do you know how so many people are
> worried about running out of money at
> retirement?
>
> Well, what I do is help them to create a
> guaranteed stream of income for the rest of
> their life.

Although a great So What Communicator
understands the importance of doing their homework
and not winging it, they also understand that every

once in awhile, you meet someone who can make a big difference in your life based on you making the right first impression. Your So What Positioning Statement helps you take advantage of these serendipitous opportunities.

TAKE-AWAY IDEAS

1. If you don't have a great answer to "What do you do for a living?," you are missing a terrific opportunity.

2. The answer to the "So what do you do?" question needs to be clear, compelling, and relevant to your audience.

3. Practice your So What Positioning Statement to the point where it sounds completely unrehearsed. Great actors constantly rehearse their lines so that their delivery appears natural and unscripted. Delivering your positioning statement should be no different.

"IT'S THE ECONOMY, STUPID."
—JAMES CARVILLE

CHAPTER 9
TIE A STRING AROUND YOUR FINGER

Now that you understand the importance of the
So What Benefit (see Chapter 5, "What's in It for
Them?"), and have determined which facet of your
product, idea, or service you want to focus on, you
might think that your work is done.

Not quite.

It turns out that determining the So What Benefit is a
good start, but it is not enough to succeed over time,
as you will see.

To make the point, let's compare and contrast the
history of two soft drinks.

The first was billed as a medicine that could help
you "recover from nervous exhaustion, loss of
manhood, and helplessness." Although it sounds like
the latest anti-depressant from one of the leading
pharmaceutical companies, it was in fact the So What
Benefit used to describe the first cola, Moxie.

Moxie Nerve Food, as it was known then, like all early
soft drinks in America, was initially intended to be a
medicine, not a refreshing beverage. Created in 1876
by Augustin Thompson in Lowell, Massachusetts,
Moxie was an enormous hit at the St. Louis World's
Fair in 1904.

By the 1920s, Moxie was the most popular soft drink in the United States—outselling both Coca-Cola and Pepsi. The word had even entered the language as a synonym for spirit or verve. (Invariably, in every movie set in the 1930s, a headstrong, independent person [usually the star] is described as "having Moxie.")

Moxie's advertising played up the drink's bitterness, stressing it was "the drink for those who are at all particular." There was a Moxie jingle, celebrity endorsements, and ever-growing sales.

So, why doesn't Moxie dominate the soft drink section of your local supermarket today?

What went wrong?

Well, when the Depression started, the Moxie Company decided to cut back on all advertising. This turned out to be a huge mistake, and Moxie began to lose market share to Coca-Cola.

Today, you can still find the occasional can of Moxie in certain stores in New England, although the company is no longer independent. It is actually owned by a local Coca-Cola bottling franchise in New England.

A once-great brand is all but forgotten.

Now, let's turn our attention to Coca-Cola, which was created a full decade after Moxie.

Atlanta pharmacist John Pemberton, who was trying to create a headache cure, mixed up the first batch of the ubiquitous soft drink in 1886. His bookkeeper, Frank Robinson, christened the invention Coca-Cola—because the soft drink's syrup contains an extract of *coca* leaves and *cola* nuts—and Robinson wrote out the name in the descriptive script we know to this day.

Coca-Cola was one of the first corporations to leverage mass media to build brand awareness and constantly remind the marketplace about its product. Robert Woodruff, the man who turned Coke into the worldwide enterprise it is today, once said he "would not rest until you could buy a Coke anywhere, anytime, and anyplace."

Woodruff, elected president of Coca-Cola in 1923 at age 33, was a marketing genius who saw opportunities for expansion everywhere. He pushed for development and distribution of the six-pack, and in 1929, Woodruff promoted a revolutionary advance: the metal, open-top cooler, which made it possible for Coca-Cola to be served ice-cold in retail outlets. By making Coca-Cola available for on-the-spot refreshment, Woodruff made it easier for people to drink Coca-Cola, whether they were at home or away, underscoring its positioning at the time as "the pause that refreshes." The tagline was a simple reminder that you would feel better by taking a break and drinking a Coke.

Every open-top cooler reinforced the distinctive red and white logo of the Coca-Cola brand. Even Coke's unique contoured, glass bottle—which is still one of the most recognizable packages on the planet—had a So What Benefit. It was recognizable even in the dark when people reached into their unlit icebox!

Over the last 125 years, part of what makes Coke so successful is that its image as the quintessential American soft drink has remained absolutely constant—with the exception of the ill-advised experiment known as New Coke.

It is the best example I know that shows you what you need to do after you have identified the So What Benefit of your product. You need to make sure your product or service is always visible and consistent, and that your So What Benefit is constantly repeated.

All this adds up to what I call the **So What Reminder**. You need to tell people often about the benefit of what you have, and you need to do this early and consistently. The fact is, in this digital age, we are all busy and have a limited attention span for anything new, even if it is something that could benefit us. As consumers, we have developed a shield of armor to help protect us from the commercial messages that bombard us by land, sea, and air. Even if we discover someone or something with a unique So What Benefit, we may forget about it; however, it's still important to remind people that our products/services continue to exist.

Coke has done this brilliantly.

Let's look at how Coca-Cola used **visibility, consistency, and repetition** to become the dominant soft drink in the world:

1. **Visibility.** You can find Coca-Cola literally everywhere in the world. Here's one simple example of how this came about. At the start of World War II, Woodruff decreed "that every man in uniform gets a bottle of Coca-Cola for five cents wherever he is, or whatever it costs the company (whichever is less)." A nickel was what John Pemberton was charging back in 1886 when he first invented the product at his pharmacy.

2. Although the Coca-Cola Company didn't earn much profit from this approach at the time, it

did gain something far more valuable—exposure throughout Europe and the Pacific from the American GIs who carried the drink with them. By the end of the war, literally millions of people in those two parts of the globe had been exposed to the soft drink. By 1960, the number of countries with Coca-Cola bottling companies had nearly doubled, and Coke had become the dominant soft drink worldwide.

3. **Consistency.** The consistent look of their bottle, and its distinctive script logo has helped imprint the connection to Coca-Cola from generation to generation. The result? A brand value, according to *Business Week* 2008, of $58 billion—*for the company's name and logo alone.*

4. **Repetition.** Yes, of course you see ads for Coca-Cola everywhere. But if all the company did were repeat the same slogan over and over again, you would quickly stop paying attention. That's why the company's marketing message changes over time—not so often as to be confusing, but often enough to keep us paying attention to the brand.

Here's an example of how Coca-Cola has continuously refreshed its advertising positioning and its slogans over time:

1886—Drink Coca-Cola.

1904—Delicious and refreshing.

1905—Coca-Cola revives and sustains.

1906—The great national temperance beverage.

1908—Good til the last drop.

1917—Three million a day.

1922—Thirst knows no season.

1923—Enjoy life.

1924—Refresh yourself.

1925—Six million a day.

1926—It had to be good to get where it is.

1927—Pure as sunlight.

1927—Around the corner from anywhere.

1928—Coca-Cola...pure drink of natural flavors.

1929—The pause that refreshes.

1932—Ice-cold sunshine.

1938—The best friend thirst ever had.

1938—Thirst asks nothing more.

1939—Coca-Cola goes along.

1939—Coca-Cola has the taste thirst goes for.

1939—Whoever you are, whatever you do, wherever you may be, when you think of refreshment, think of ice-cold Coca-Cola.

1942—The only thing like Coca-Cola is Coca-Cola itself.

1948—Where there's Coke there's hospitality.

1952—What you want is a Coke.

1956—Coca-Cola…makes good things taste better.

1957—Sign of good taste.

1958—The cold, crisp taste of Coke.

1959—Be really refreshed.

1963—Things go better with Coke.

1969—It's the real thing.

1975—Look up America. (U.S. only)

1976—Coke adds life.

1979—Have a Coke and a smile.

1982—Coke is it!

1985—America's real choice. (U.S. only)

1986—Red, white, & you. (For Coca-Cola Classic)

1986—Catch the wave. (For New Coke)

1987—You can't beat the feeling.

1990—Can't beat the real thing. (U.S. and Canada only)

1993—Always Coca-Cola.

2000—Enjoy.

2001—Life tastes good.

2003—Real. (U.S. and Canada only)

2003—Make it real. (UK and Republic of Ireland only)

2003—As it should be. (Australia and New Zealand only)

2006—The Coke side of life.

2008—Brrrrr.

In contrast, Moxie did not employ a So What Reminder strategy. As part of its cost-cutting during tough economic times, the company also cut back on distribution to concentrate on its core markets and, although the product remained consistent, no one knew about it, because it slashed its advertising and promotion budget. As happens all too often to companies that apply this knee-jerk approach when hit with hard times, Moxie entered a death spiral from which the company never emerged.

You simply cannot starve yourself to corporate success. Coke proved that. Its willingness to boldly expand their marketing and promotion during the worst economic depression of the twentieth century set the stage for them to reap huge dividends and become the industry leader. And it wasn't just Coke. Other leading companies, like General Electric and Procter & Gamble, not only survived, but came out of that economic cycle as the industry leader.

YOU MUST REMEMBER THIS

One of the ironies of the free enterprise system is that once a company achieves dominance, it often loses the entrepreneurial spirit of innovation and desire for constant improvement that made it successful initially. It becomes, as the vernacular puts it, "fat, dumb, and happy."

The So What Reminder forces you to refine, refresh, and renew the way you think and communicate about what you do or sell so that it continues to be relevant in an ever-changing world.

Let's review a few examples where the So What Reminder helped make a difference in the success of the idea or product.

Politics

In what may be the best-known illustration of the So What Reminder, political consultant James Carville hung up a sign at headquarters to remind everyone working on the presidential campaign of Bill Clinton that the So What Benefit they were selling to voters in the 1992 election was, "It's the economy, stupid."

It would have been very easy to get "off message" and start talking about a wide range of subjects— everything from international diplomacy to race relations. Instead, Carville's simple strategy helped the campaign team stay tightly focused on its key So What Benefit, which was improving the economy, based on new ideas from a new administration.

Religion

Although it's easy to criticize the failures of the great religions of our time, the fact is we can still learn a lot from institutions that in some cases have survived for thousands of years. Some of the most powerful religious communicators, like Billy Graham and Dr. Martin Luther King, Jr., understood intuitively how to take an old idea and make it new and relevant again.

In listening to one of Dr. King's recorded speeches, he tells the familiar biblical story of the Good Samaritan. At first, I wondered if that parable from 2,000 years ago, which calls upon all of us to have compassion for our neighbors, had any relevance in today's world. Dr. King gave the story a new perspective and meaning by saying that the story of the Good Samaritan was really about changing the questions we ask ourselves. For example, instead of asking, "What will happen to me if I help this person?," the Good Samaritan asks, "What will happen to this person if I don't help him?"

Dr. King reminded his audience—using an old, familiar story—that they were faced with the same dilemma that existed for the Good Samaritan more than 2,000 years earlier. Every week in services around the world, religious leaders practice the So What Reminder by refreshing an ancient idea in a new context so that it is relevant for their modern audience.

Don't underestimate the power of reminding people of different facets of the same message week after week, month after month, and year after year to keep it relevant.

Fast Food

Two all-beef patties, special sauce, lettuce, cheese, pickles, onions, on a sesame seed bun. Originally, the ingredients appeared as a one-word (TwoAllBeef PattiesSpecialSauceLettuceCheesePicklesOnions-OnASesameSeedBun) headline for a McDonald's ad developed for college newspapers. The advertising concept was to purposely turn the ingredients into a tongue twister. The jingle first appeared in a TV commercial titled "In a Word," which only ran for 18 months in 1975 and 1976, but remains memorable nearly 30 years later.

What do these three examples have in common?

A relentless focus on reminding their target audiences about the So What Benefit of the candidate, message, or product in question. Repetition is a must. You just can't expect that the So What Benefit of what you are offering will get through to your audience the first time you mention it. Folks may not be paying attention. And even if they are, there are very few things we hear once and remember forever.

Using the strategy of visibility, consistency, and repetition will help remind your target audience about your So What Benefit over time.

Look back over the last 12 months. What have you done to keep "the string" wrapped around your customer's finger?

TAKE-AWAY IDEAS

1. The So What Reminder is the process of refining, refreshing, and renewing both the way you think and communicate about what you do or sell so that it continues to be relevant even as times and circumstances change.

2. Moxie soda stopped reminding people why they should drink its product; Coca-Cola didn't—using visibility, consistency, and repetition brilliantly. Which soft drink are you more likely to have in your refrigerator?

3. To apply the So What Reminder, determine if your message is still relevant, and if so, make sure you harness the power of this strategy to ensure it remains that way.

"A NEW IDEA IS FIRST
CONDEMNED AS
RIDICULOUS AND
THEN DISMISSED AS
TRIVIAL UNTIL FINALLY
IT BECOMES WHAT
EVERYONE KNOWS."
—WILLIAM JAMES

CHAPTER 10
**GETTING FROM WHERE YOU ARE
TO WHERE YOU WANT TO BE**

On September 12, 1962, President John F. Kennedy declared the following:

> "We choose to go to the moon in this decade…not because it is easy but because it is hard. Because that goal will serve to organize and measure the best of our energies and skills, because that challenge is one that we are willing to accept; one we are unwilling to postpone and one we intend to win."

With these words, President Kennedy announced his desire to land a man on the moon and bring him safely back to earth before the end of the decade.

When he delivered this speech at Rice University in Houston, the United States was still reeling from the Soviet Union's pulling ahead in the space race. The Russians had, in 1957, launched Sputnik, an unmanned satellite, and four years later, they sent the first man into space.

In President Kennedy's message, he used the So What Filter to think in terms of why the citizens of the United States would be interested in investing their time, energy, and enormous financial resources—$25 billion in 1962 or around $175 billion in 2008—in sending an American to the moon.

When President Kennedy said, "we choose to go to the moon," only one American had ever even successfully orbited the Earth, and even he, John Glenn, hadn't done it for very long. Glenn's *Friendship 7* spacecraft only completed three earth orbits on February 20, 1962, and the flight was over in less than five hours.

Many NASA employees doubted whether Kennedy's ambitious goal could be met. But by brilliantly equating the success of the space program with national pride, the President was able to provide a So What Benefit in answer to the question of why America should make the investment to go to the moon.

In short, Kennedy understood the power of appealing to people's emotions versus trying to convince them with logic about why the rock samples that would be brought back to earth would matter to anyone other than a few geologists. That is why he stressed the emotional component of the space program—the pride we could all take in accomplishing the seemingly impossible—and not the tangible.

He further understood that achieving this goal not only gave America bragging rights, but also would send a powerful message to the rest of the world, even the part that was behind the Iron Curtain, about what we were capable of and what's possible in a free, democratic society.

President Kennedy also understood the So What Reminder. He knew it was not enough to talk about the goal of sending a man to the moon only once and think that the entire country would get behind it. For example, NASA launched a massive public relations campaign that turned astronauts into rock stars. The media was invited inside the astronauts' training program, so that the public could see first-hand what the preparation was like.

All this effort culminated July 20, 1969 when, as NASA puts it with justifiable pride: "The human race accomplished its single greatest technological achievement of all time when a human first set foot on another celestial body."

So, what does this mean to you? Even though President Kennedy didn't live to see the realization of this dream, as a So What Communicator, he demonstrated how a new mindset created the leadership, confidence, and direction America needed to make the impossible possible.

As we move further into the twenty-first century, your ability to give your audience leadership, confidence, and direction about their future is no less critical than

it was in President Kennedy's day. By using the So
What Mindset to clarify your thinking, you will have
a process to help you communicate what matters
most to your audience based on what you want to
accomplish.

President Kennedy did not ask America if he thought
going to the moon was a goal they were interested
in voting for. Rather, he decided as a leader and
commander-in-chief, he would demonstrate that
this was something important to do, and it would
ultimately benefit all of us.

If President Kennedy had lacked the ability
to transform his vision for the future into a
communication that resonated with the American
people, he may have ended up like so many people
who are ignorant of the So What Mindset: He could
have seen a bold idea go absolutely nowhere.

21-DAY CHALLENGE

President Kennedy had help from a number of
"coaches"—speechwriters, political advisors, and his
brothers (one the U.S. Attorney General and the other
soon to be a U.S. Senator)—to frame his message in
a way that would resonate with his target market: the
American people.

I have had coaches who helped me develop my habits of thinking in a new way.

And in turn, I am here to coach you in adopting the strategies from *So What? How to Communicate What Really Matters to Your Audience* to help you communicate the ideas you have in a way that connects with your audience.

It has been said that, "only the mediocre are always at their best." If you've read this far, it is clear that mediocrity and complacency are not acceptable for you.

What to Do Now

Most people understand that it takes 21 days of consistent reinforcement to establish a new idea or habit. As a reader of *So What? How to Communicate What Really Matters to Your Audience*, I am inviting you to join our community and participate in a 21-day challenge. This opportunity requires you to invest two minutes a day for the next 21 days to read a short passage or watch a brief video designed to reinforce one of the key concepts from this book to recondition your thinking and help you develop the So What Mindset.

You can participate in this challenge by signing up for a daily email reminder that will be sent to you every day for 21 days; visit sowhatbook.com for more details.

Like President Kennedy, developing this mindset will help you transform your big ideas, even those deemed "impossible," and make them a reality because you know how to engage the talents of other people by showing them what's in it for them. Best of all, after 21 days, this new approach will become effortless because by that point, it will be an unconscious, but integral, part of your thinking.

A FINAL THOUGHT

I leave you with the words of Ralph Waldo Emerson, someone who had a clear understanding of *So What? How to Communicate What Really Matters to Your Audience.* He said:

"IT IS ONE OF THE BEAUTIFUL COMPENSATIONS OF LIFE THAT NO MAN CAN SINCERELY TRY TO HELP ANOTHER WITHOUT HELPING HIMSELF."

TAKE-AWAY IDEAS

1. Find a So What Benefit in what you are promoting or selling. President Kennedy found a So What Benefit (that is, national pride) to answer the question of why America should make the investment to go to the moon.

2. Use a So What Reminder to keep your audience engaged. President Kennedy used the So What Reminder to turn astronauts into rock stars and get the public involved.

3. Enlist the help of "coaches" to leverage your strength and minimize your weaknesses. President Kennedy had help from a number of coaches to frame his message in a way that would resonate with the American people.

In the Chinese language, the symbol for crisis is often depicted with characters that represent both danger and opportunity.

That thought came to mind recently, since from almost anyone's point of view, the stock market meltdown of 2008, which was part of the worst recession we have experienced in more than 70 years, certainly qualifies as a crisis. And although it's true that this change poses a danger to us individually and collectively, it also represents a tremendous opportunity.

What you have read in this book is designed to help you become indispensable in any economic cycle. If anything, the lessons are even more important during a downturn.

In Chapter 9, "Tie a String Around Your Finger," I discussed how Moxie cut costs during the Great Depression, while Coke continued to practice visibility, consistency, and repetition. Moxie is now a footnote in the history of the nation's soft drinks, whereas Coke continues to thrive.

So What? A Final Word

Well, I am watching a reprise of Coke's approach during our current economic woes. In 2008, as the recession continued to worsen, Coke took a bold step and, at the Beijing Summer Olympics, made a significant investment that began the process of introducing more than 1.3 billion people in China to their product. Part of their challenge was that most people in China do not drink their beverages cold but rather at room temperature or warm. Coke recognized that in order for their product to become accepted, they had to shift this cultural norm by introducing people at the Olympics to the concept of an ice-cold Coke. Constant repetition, and visibility throughout the games, helped position Coke for success. By the time the Olympics were over, according to a *Wall Street Journal* article, 43 percent of Chinese people knew that Coke sponsored the games. Just 3 percent of the Chinese could name another sponsor.

Coke has not let up. In another bold move in January 2009, the *Journal* reported, "Coke Bets on Russia for Sales Even as Economy Falls Flat." According to Muhtar Kent, Coca-Cola's Chief Executive Officer, "Times like these are not an excuse to sit back and ride out the storm." Although the recession has battered many companies around the world, Coke represents the flip side of the downturn: businesses that have held up relatively well and plan to expand their empires during this period of uncertainty.

As you can see, some 75 years later, Kent is borrowing from the playbook created by an earlier CEO, Robert Woodruff. In stepping up the company's marketing with visibility, consistency, and repetition, when times are tough, he is positioning the company for success when the economy turns around.

With that in mind:

- ▶ Are you following the playbook from Moxie or from Coke?

- ▶ What can you be doing to demonstrate the visibility, consistency, and repetition of your message?

- ▶ With your competition cutting back, is it time for you to act boldly?

The Coke experience shows that there is no new magic bullet. The simple fact is that you need to invest your time and energy answering the So What Question over and over again to the point where it becomes a habit. The opportunities for you are greater now than before because there is a changing of the guard at many companies around the world. Many of the old relationships and barriers that once kept you out have effectively fallen. (And, of course, the people you have worked with in the past may no longer be in the same position either, meaning you will have to explain anew why the company should do business with you.)

This means that now, more than ever, you need to hone your So What Message, and that means constant *deliberate practice.*

It's a concept that Geoffrey Colvin captured perfectly in a *Fortune* magazine article titled, "What It Takes to Be Great."

Colvin correctly pointed out that there is a difference between practice and what the best performers do—something he describes as "deliberate practice." "It's activity that is explicitly intended to improve performance, that reaches for objectives just beyond one's level of competence, provides feedback on results, and involves high levels of repetition."

For example, Colvin said, "Simply hitting a bucket of balls is not deliberate practice, which is why most golfers don't get better. Hitting an eight iron 300 times with a goal of leaving the ball within 20 feet of the pin 80 percent of the time while continually observing results and making appropriate adjustments, and doing that for hours every day—that's deliberate practice."

You need to engage in deliberate practice when it comes to working on your So What Message, especially during tough times. (Re-read the "21-Day Challenge" section in Chapter 10, "Getting from Where You Are to Where You Want to Be," for one way to go about it. On sowhatbook.com, you will also find video clips and training tools that support the proven, key ideas from this book and make it easier for you to incorporate the So What Mindset into your daily routine.)

So What? How to Communicate What Matters Most to Your Audience can also form the foundation of your own internal training program. For example, you can purchase a copy of the book for each of your direct reports, and then on a weekly basis, take one of the ideas and make it the focus of a team meeting.

For example, in Week 1, you might ask: How do we develop the So What Mindset as an organization?

In Week 2: What is the So What Benefit we offer?

In Week 3: How do we ensure that everything we do passes the So What Test?

In Week 4: How do we get our audience engaged with the So What Positioning Statement?

In Week 5: How do we create a So What Reminder—like Coca-Cola—for our product and service?

You get the idea. Mastering the So What Mindset can definitely help you become indispensable to your clients and your customers, regardless of the current economic cycle.

The words of Jeff Goldberg, who passed away in January 2008, still resonate in my mind: "Some people make it happen, some watch it happen, and some wonder what happened."

Your goal is to be one of the people who makes things happen.

"EVERYTHING SHOULD BE MADE AS SIMPLE AS POSSIBLE BUT NOT SIMPLER."
—ALBERT EINSTEIN

GLOSSARY

benefit—The benefit of your product or service that causes your audience to respond with "I love it, I need it, I'll buy it."

biography (personal)—A written document about you that describes the benefit you bring to your clients and customers that will solve their problem, answer their questions about who you are, your qualifications, and what makes you unique. It is not a resume. It is often used to help set the stage or position your value.

communicator—A person who understands that what you do before and after your presentation may be as important as what you do during your presentation; the foundational principle for a So What Communicator is remaining authentic to yourself.

CSI research—The process of finding relevant information about your audience that can help you create the right questions to ask so that you can begin to understand what matters most to them.

filter—An internal mental process that acts like a polarized lens, helping you to see what others might miss, even though it is right in front of their eyes.

grabber opening—Opening of any presentation that is designed to grab your audience's attention.

ideal client profile—A process that helps to clarify the kinds of people that can most benefit from what you do.

introduction (card)—The 30-second introduction, derived from your personal written biography, is a written documentation to help set the stage and introduce you properly in front of an audience. It typically ends with the phrase, "please join me in welcoming…." It does not include as much information as your personal biography.

It's About Them, Not You—The quickest way to reduce nervousness is to focus on the needs of your audience rather than be concerned about how you look or sound in front of the audience.

matrix—The process of asking "For What?," "So What?," and "Now What?" to prepare your presentation.

mindset—The habit of asking yourself the So What Question before beginning any communication.

orchestration—The organization of any situation or event unobtrusively, so that a desired effect or outcome is achieved. See *winging it*.

ostensible benefit—A benefit that might appear to be true, but is not necessarily the case.

positioning statement—A clear, compelling, and relevant answer to the questions "What do you do?" or "How can you help me?."

psychic real estate—The words, pictures, and feelings people associate with a product or service.

question—The process of asking yourself what benefit your audience receives from what you are communicating. Remember to begin at the big question level (30,000 feet) versus starting with a tactical question (sea level).

reminder—The process of refining, refreshing, and renewing both the way you think and the way you communicate about what you do or sell so that it continues to be relevant, even as times and circumstances change.

setting the stage—The process of planning the first impression you make on your audience.

So What Test—Every single time you communicate, you must ask yourself what's important to your audience. Have you thought about the key points of your presentation from their perspective or could they be saying, "So what?"

undeniable truth—A statement that almost everyone could agree with that has the natural effect of causing people to nod their heads in agreement.

visibility, consistency, and repetition—A focused strategy used to remind your audience about the So What Benefit of the candidate, message, or product in question. Repetition is a must.

winging it— To make up what you are going to say in real time. This phrase originates from the theatrical slang sense of an actor learning his lines in the wings before going on stage or else not learning them at all and being fed by a prompter in the wings. See *orchestration*.

I want to thank the many people—clients, partners, friends, and family—who have gone the extra mile to help me transform this idea into a reality.

To the clients of Insight Development Group, Inc.—all have made a contribution to making this idea better. In particular:

- ▶ Noel Anderson and Pat Kane for making our boot camps a reality

- ▶ Andy Reiss and Al Cohn for helping me spread my message near and far

- ▶ Ed Cosgrove for keeping the "fire burning"

- ▶ Al Martella for helping me understand the power of listening before speaking

- ▶ George Veazey and Jon Taylor for demonstrating grace under pressure

- ▶ Laura Palmer, Brian Nelson, and Chris Bilello for demonstrating the importance of the So What Reminder regardless of the economic climate

ACKNOWLEDGMENTS

To the Pacific Life Management Team—Jim Morris, Bill Robinson, Dewey Bushaw, Chris Van Mierlo, Bob Bruno, John White, Stuart Holland, Jack Hunter, George Paulik, Paul Croxton, Mike Curry, George McFadden, Mark Johnson, Vince Spera, Bruce McKibbin, Kevin Berwald, Mike Miranne, Chris Ratchford, and Brad Armstrong—thanks for the opportunity to help change one small part of the world with So What thinking.

To my friends and advisors—Craig Bandes, Doug Dubiel, Michael Elkin, John Evans, Tony Jeary, Rob Kiltz, Lisa Knox, John Lotka, Frank Maselli, Donald Moine, Alan Parisse, John Peterson, Tomas Pineda, Shannah Poccini, Trent Smock, Dan Sullivan, Dan Taylor, Brian Tracy, and Ami Tully-Lotka—thanks for your feedback, pushback, and encouragement along the way.

To Neil Wood—whose enthusiasm, attitude, and Olympic mindset have taught me about the power of perseverance and that life is a marathon and not a sprint.

To my Forum One Group—Bill Kazman, Yuchun Lee, John Miller, Marty Murphy, Cris Peterson, Mario Ricciardelli, Matt Rosenthal, Eric Silverman—this great group of young entrepreneurs has inspired me every month for more than a decade with their dedication, insight, and humor.

To my family—Kristen, Cole, and Grace, who gave me a chance to practice what I preach—thank you for your unconditional support and endless encouragement.

To my father, Robert Magnacca, my mother and stepfather, Diana and Dene Truax, my brother, Scott Magnacca, and my mother-in-law, Ginger Nehring— thanks for your help and support along the way and for helping me believe that anything is possible.

To my Agent—John Willig—who persevered until it was done.

To my Editor—Jennifer Simon and the Pearson/FT Press team—thanks for your direction and ability to keep asking better questions.

To the Insight Development Team—Paul B. Brown, Eric Delin, Diane Donnelly, Jonathan Follett, Eleanor Uddo and Dave Yoken—thanks for all you do to help make our ideas a reality.

Last but not least, to my assistant—Annie Taber— whose creativity, attention to detail, endless patience, and beautiful lakeside office made the writing of this book so much easier.

NUMBERS

A

B

C